LEVERAGED
ESOPs
AND EMPLOYEE BUYOUTS

Sixth Edition

LEVERAGED
ESOPs
AND EMPLOYEE BUYOUTS

Sixth Edition

Vaughn Gordy • Neal Hawkins • Mary Josephs • William Merten
Rebecca Miller • Scott Rodrick • Corey Rosen • John Solimine

The National Center for Employee Ownership
Oakland, California

Leveraged ESOPs and Employee Buyouts, Sixth Edition

Book design by Scott Rodrick.

Copyright © 2013 by The National Center for Employee Ownership. All rights reserved. No part of this book may be reproduced or transmitted in any form or by any means, electronic or mechanical, including photocopying, recording, or by any information storage and retrieval system, without prior written permission from the publisher.

First edition 1997. Second edition 1999. Third edition 2000. Fourth edition 2001. Fifth edition 2005, reprinted with corrections 2009. Sixth edition April 2013.

The National Center for Employee Ownership
1736 Franklin Street, 8th Floor
Oakland, CA 94612
(510) 208-1300
(510) 272-9510 (fax)
Web site: www.nceo.org

ISBN: 978-1-938220-06-7

Contents

Preface   vii

Part 1: Legal, Valuation, and Accounting Considerations

1. A Primer on Leveraged ESOPs   3
   Corey Rosen

2. Understanding ESOP Valuation   31
   Corey Rosen

3. Accounting for ESOP Transactions   51
   Rebecca J. Miller

4. Section 1042 and the Tax-Deferred ESOP "Rollover"   77
   Scott Rodrick

5. Using ESOPs in Mergers and Acquisitions   99
   William Merten and Vaughn Gordy

Part 2: Financing

6. The Changing Faces of ESOP Financing   117
   Mary Josephs

7. ESOP Underwriting Considerations   121
   Mary Josephs and Neal Hawkins

8. Mature ESOP Considerations   151
   Mary Josephs and Neal Hawkins

9. Types of Capital   157
   Neal Hawkins and John Solimine

10. Providers of Capital   173
    Neal Hawkins and John Solimine

11. Seller Financing   179
    Mary Josephs and Neal Hawkins

   Appendix: Financial Glossary   189
   Mary Josephs and Neal Hawkins

About the Authors   197

About the NCEO   201

Preface

Leveraged ESOPs...

During the past several decades, employee stock ownership plans (ESOPs) have become a familiar feature on the U.S. business landscape. There are currently almost 11,000 companies with ESOPs; many of these ESOPs are leveraged, meaning that the ESOP has borrowed money on the credit of the employer or other related parties to buy company stock. It is the only qualified employee benefit plan that can do this. Moreover, the company can deduct ESOP contributions it makes for both principal and interest payments on the loan. This tax-advantaged leveraging capability, in conjunction with other tax advantages, makes the ESOP an ideal vehicle for several purposes, including buying out a company; divesting a subsidiary, division, or product line; enabling a public company to repurchase shares; restructuring existing benefit plans; and acquiring capital with a low-cost loan.

...and Employee Buyouts

A leveraged ESOP can be the ideal vehicle for an employee buyout. In the past several decades, thousands of companies have been established through selling a company to an ESOP or through corporate divestitures to newly created companies that are at least partially ESOP-owned. If a broad-based group of employees buys out a company or division, they will probably use a leveraged ESOP to do it. Hence, although there is no chapter in this book titled "Employee Buyouts," every chapter concerns issues to consider in an ESOP-based employee buyout.

About This Book

ESOPs are complicated mechanisms, and using leverage increases their complexity. This book is designed to be a practical tool for anyone dealing with that complexity, whether the leveraged ESOP will purchase a small amount of stock or be used for an employee buyout of part or all of a company. Business owners, managers, their advisors, lenders, and others interested in employee ownership plans will all find this book helpful. It covers not only financing, accounting, and other aspects of the transaction but also the rules for the tax-deferred "rollover" for a selling owner in a closely held C corporation under Section 1042 of the Internal Revenue Code.

About the Sixth Edition

The first edition of *Leveraged ESOPs and Employee Buyouts* appeared in 1997. In the sixth edition (2013), the book has been split into two parts. Part 1 updates several chapters on legal and accounting issues from previous editions and adds new chapters on valuation and mergers and acquisitions. Part 2 is devoted to vastly expanded coverage of the intricacies of ESOP transaction financing, beginning with an overview of the current environment and ending with a glossary of terms.

Part 1

Legal, Valuation, and Accounting Considerations

Chapter 1

A Primer on Leveraged ESOPs

Corey Rosen

Owners of closely held companies who want to sell their businesses to employees face a problem. The employees might be willing, but their wallets are probably not. Buying shares in a company is an expensive and risky proposition, and it all must be done in after-tax dollars. One solution would be for the employees to borrow the money to buy the company and repay it out of future corporate profits, but those funds would not be tax-deductible and the loans could be very hard to acquire. Fortunately, an employee stock ownership plan (ESOP) provides a very practical solution, one that is funded not directly by employees, but out of future pretax corporate profits. An ESOP not only is more tax-efficient than a direct purchase for employees but, if certain rules are met, can provide the seller with a tax deferral on the gain if the company is a C corporation. Banks have been willing to loan to these plans if provided adequate collateral, while sellers can also take back a note and earn a competitive rate of interest. ESOPs started in the 1950s on a case-by-case IRS approval basis, and then became part of the Employee Retirement Income Security Act of 1974 (ERISA). ESOPs were specifically created to make it possible for ordinary employees to become owners of their companies through an employer-sponsored trust that receives corporate contributions of stock or cash to buy stock. ESOPs also were given the right, unique among employee benefit plans, to borrow money to buy company shares, money the company repays out of future deductible contributions. Most of the time, these ESOP loans are for business transition purposes, but companies can and do also use the borrowing capacity of ESOPs to buy other assets (including other companies) using pretax dollars, as well as for other corporate finance purposes.

ESOPs have borrowed hundreds of billions of dollars to buy stock in their companies since 1974. The simple idea behind ESOPs is that if Congress provided tax incentives to owners of existing businesses to provide collateral to back up ESOP loans, either by pledging corporate or personal assets, business owners would be more likely to share ownership with their employees.

In return for the substantial tax benefits this book describes for ESOPs, Congress insisted on some rules. "ESOPs must be fair," it decreed, creating a set of rules to define just what "fair" means. What follows here is an introduction to all these benefits and rules. Complex as they can be, however, the core concept is simple: ESOPs are a way to use the future earnings of the corporation to acquire ownership for employees. Tax benefits and, hopefully, the employees themselves help provide the added economic value to generate these additional earnings. In return for the tax benefits, companies must comply with rules designed to make sure the plans are rigorous enough to really provide benefits to employees, but not so rigorous that no company would set them up. The complexity of the laws is something that can easily be handled by professional advisors; people in companies just need to know the essential outlines.

What Is an ESOP?

An ESOP is a kind of employee benefit plan. ESOPs were given a specific statutory framework in 1974 with the enactment of ERISA and were the subject of new legislation, mostly to add benefits, in almost every Congress between 1974 and 1986, with some additional laws since then. Like other tax-qualified deferred compensation plans under Section 401(a) of the Internal Revenue Code (the "Code"), such as profit sharing plans and pensions, ESOPs must be operated for "the exclusive benefit of plan participants." This does not mean exactly what it says, though. It does not mean that other people cannot benefit from ESOPs, because no one would set them up were that the case. It does mean that when the interests of the participants of the plan conflict with the interests of people outside the plan, the participants should be paramount. Moreover, ESOPs must be operated by a trustee in a manner that is prudent and in compliance with the fiduciary rules of ERISA. Buying stock in the ESOP's sponsor when you, as trustee, know the company is about to encounter severe problems, for instance, is not prudent. Finally, ESOPs, like other qualified deferred compensation plans, must not discriminate in their operations in favor of highly compensated employees, officers, and owners. As was said of the Golden Rule, "all the rest is commentary."

Technically, an ESOP is a stock bonus plan qualified to borrow money. Whereas stock bonus plans are only required to distribute their benefits in the form of employer securities but can hold any mix of investments they like while people are still in the plan, ESOPs are required to invest primarily in employer stock. While there is no regulation about what "primarily" means, most ESOP specialists think it is over 50%. The percentage probably can temporarily drop below that from time to time, perhaps even for a year or two, and the rest of the assets can be invested in any sound investments. ESOPs can also start off by just receiving cash contributions from the company that are intended to buy stock later. Again, there is no consensus on how long an ESOP can do this, but doing it for two or three years seems safe.

How Leveraged ESOPs Work

Essentially, a leveraged ESOP is an intermediary in a loan transaction. Rather than borrow the money directly, a company borrows money and reloans it to an ESOP.

The company first sets up a employee stock ownership trust. The trust then borrows money to acquire stock in the company. The stock can be shares already owned, treasury shares, or new shares issued specifically for sale to the ESOP. Proceeds from the loan can be used for any legitimate business purpose. The stock is put into a "suspense account," where it is released to employee accounts as the loan is repaid. After employees leave the company or retire, the company distributes the stock in their account, which it must offer to repurchase at fair market value if the company is closely held. In the typical ESOP transaction, the lender will loan to the company, which reloans the money to the ESOP. Provided certain rules are followed, this "inside" loan does not have to be on the same terms as the "outside" loan. Lenders prefer loaning directly to the company, but the accounting and tax effects of this two-step process are essentially the same as if the loan were made directly to the ESOP.

In return for agreeing to borrow through the ESOP, the company receives significant tax benefits, provided it follows the rules to assure employees are treated fairly. First, the company can deduct the entire loan contribution it makes to the ESOP, within certain payroll-based limits described below. That means the company, in effect, can deduct interest and principal on the loan, not just interest. Second, the company, if a C corporation, can deduct dividends paid on the shares acquired with the proceeds of the loan that are used to repay the loan itself (in other words, the earnings of the stock being acquired help pay for stock itself). Again, there are limits, as described below in sections on the rules of the loan and contribution limits. Sellers to qualifying ESOPs in C corporations can defer capital gains taxes on the sale. While S corporations do not get this same tax benefit, any profits attributable to the ESOP are not subject to federal and, almost always, state income tax. Thus, whereas an S corporation normally pays distributions to shareholders to fund their tax bills, a 100% ESOP-owned S corporation generally has no tax bills to fund because the ESOP is not taxed.

Uses of Leveraged ESOPs

An ESOP can borrow money for any business purpose. The most common of these is to buy out shares of an existing owner in a closely held C corporation. Under Section 1042 of the Code, a company can set up an ESOP and have it borrow money to buy shares from an existing owner. If the ESOP owns at least 30% of the shares in the company after that transaction, that sale, plus any subsequent sales, qualifies the seller to reinvest the proceeds in securities of U.S. operating companies and defer tax on the gain made from the sale to the ESOP until these replacement investments are sold. This tax benefit applies only to closely held C corporations; the seller must be an individual, an estate, one of certain trusts, a partnership, or an S corporation. Shares must have been held for at least three years (if the ownership form changes, such as from a partnership to an S corporation, the ownership of the shares in the new entity "tacks" onto the shares of the old one).

While this is the most common application of a leveraged ESOP, it is only one of several potential uses. For instance, an ESOP can be used to buy another company, an increasingly common application.

Because contributions to the ESOP to repay the loan are tax-deductible, the acquisition can be made in pretax dollars. In this application, a company can, for instance, print new shares or issue treasury shares to sell to an ESOP, which borrows money to acquire them. Then the company uses the loan proceeds to purchase the target and repays the loan with tax-deductible contributions to the ESOP. Alternatively, the acquiring company could do a tax-free stock-for-stock merger with the target. Then the ESOP could borrow money to buy out the shares (now shares of the acquiring company) from the owners of the target. The acquirer can also finance the establishment of an ESOP in the target, which buys the owner's shares. Then the two ESOPs are merged and the target company dissolved. If both companies are closely held C corporations, as explained in the chapter on mergers and acquisitions, it is possible to structure this transaction so that if it meets the rules for the tax-deferred rollover described above, the seller or sellers can qualify for a tax deferral of gains on the sale.

Another application for a leveraged ESOP is to acquire new capital. Any ESOP, whether in a C or S corporation, or a public or closely held corporation, can use an ESOP this way. Here, the company issues new shares or treasury shares and sells them to the ESOP, which borrows the funds to acquire the stock. The sale proceeds then are used to acquire new machinery, buildings, inventory, or any other property that might otherwise be financed. The company can then repay the loan through the ESOP in pretax dollars. Of course, this will have the impact of diluting other shareholders, but it also provides an employee benefit at the same time it is financing growth more efficiently. A similar approach can be used to refinance debt. Public companies also use leveraged ESOPs to buy back shares from the market.

ESOPs are also commonly used in divestitures of subsidiaries. Here, a new acquisition corporation is established. It sets up an ESOP for the employees of the entity being sold. The acquisition company ("Newco") then borrows money, which it reloans to the ESOP, to enable the ESOP to buy newly issued shares in Newco. Newco uses the money from the sale to buy assets for the parent and then repays the ESOP loan out of future revenues.

In all these transactions, it is possible and sometimes necessary to combine the ESOP purchase with equity investments from managers, outsiders, or even the employees themselves. These investments do not count as ESOP ownership, however, when calculating tax benefits. For instance, if an ESOP buys 30% of a company and managers 20%, the seller in a C corporation can defer taxes only of the sale of the 30% to the ESOP.

Finally, leveraged ESOPs are often done in stages so that the company does not have the burden of repaying excessive debt all at once.

Setting Up a Leveraged ESOP

The Trust

Setting up a leveraged ESOP raises several issues. First, what is a trust? Generally speaking, a trust is an arrangement whereby property is transferred to a "trustee" who administers it for the benefit of a designated beneficiary. In particular, an ESOP trust is a legal entity that holds property, mainly company stock contributed by the employer or bought with funds contributed by the employer, for the ESOP's participants. Like other trusts, the ESOP trust is designed to protect its beneficiaries. A trustee is appointed to do this. The ESOP trustee must ensure that the shares are valued properly, must vote the shares (often based on directions from the board or an ESOP committee, but some companies have independent trustees and others allow employees to direct the trustees), must ensure that employee accounts are properly maintained, and must otherwise attend to the rules of ESOPs and the plan document.

To help assure independence, many ESOP companies appoint bank trust departments or other trust companies to serve this function. Other companies appoint managers or other insiders as trustees. The law does not prohibit insiders from acting as trustees, despite their potential conflict of interest. If a conflict should arise, however, and the ESOP, the company's board, and other at-risk parties are brought to court, the presence of an independent trustee may weigh in the company's favor.

Who Can Be Lenders

Just about anyone can lend the ESOP money, including commercial lenders, sellers, and the company itself. ESOPs can also issue bonds to raise money, although this has been rare in recent years and is limited to the largest transactions. When a "party-in-interest" such as the seller or the company makes a loan, the terms of the loan must be not less favorable than an arm's length transaction (that is, similar to what might be available from a commercial lender facing comparable risks).

When a seller lends to an ESOP, this can be in an installment sale. If the company is a C corporation and the ESOP ends up with at least 30% of the company's stock, the seller can still qualify for one of the main benefits of an ESOP, the ability to defer taxation on gains made from the sale by reinvesting in qualified replacement investments. Only amounts reinvested during the period from 3 months before to 12 months after the sale qualify, however. The sellers cannot simply keep reinvesting and rolling over their installment payments. The seller can reinvest an amount up to the entire value of the sale, however, by using other funds. One popular approach addresses this problem by allowing sellers to buy long-term bonds with the loan proceeds. A broker would sell bonds equal in value to the note; the seller would use the first installment of the note as a down payment and borrow the rest from a bank using the bond as collateral.

Seller financing has become very popular in recent years. Sellers can structure the notes at rates similar to what a commercial lender would charge. In some cases, sellers also take warrants (the right to purchase a certain number of shares at the price the ESOP pays but for some number of years into the future) in return for lower interest rates. Companies buy back the warrants before they expire so the seller does not end up with stock again. Either way, the seller gets a rate of return on the note that is likely to be more than what other investments would yield and gets the principal purchased over time as well.

How the Money Is Borrowed

In the simplest form, the ESOP borrows the money directly, then uses it to buy company shares. The company then makes contributions to the ESOP to repay the loan. The ESOP may pledge the stock as collateral, but the company almost always must guarantee the loan with something more persuasive (assets or earnings). In addition, in many cases where the seller is reinvesting in qualified replacement property, the lender asks for part or all of these securities as collateral. Generally, as the loan is repaid, that portion of the collateral is released.

In practice, most loans are actually made to the company, which relends the money to the ESOP on the same or similar terms. Most lenders (including sellers) prefer to lend to the company. That way, they have better access to collateral and the company's cash flow, and fewer potential legal conflicts. The company can, however, make its loan to the ESOP on different terms than its loan from the lender, provided the transaction is an arm's length equivalent and the new terms of the loan to the ESOP meet fiduciary concerns (this is described in more detail below).

What Company Stock Can Be Used

ESOP rules are very strict on what qualifies as company stock. In closely held companies, the ESOP loan can only acquire stock with the highest combination of voting and dividend rights, or preferred stock readily convertible into such stock. In practice, that means ESOPs acquire either voting common stock or convertible preferred stock. In public companies, the ESOP can acquire any kind of common stock that is publicly traded. While the shares almost always must be voting shares, who votes them and how is more complex than it seems (it is not necessarily the employees). This is discussed in detail below.

In using preferred shares, it is important to make sure that the capitalization structure is not unfavorable to employee interests. Preferred shares whose upside potential is capped in value, for instance, are not considered in the employees' best interest. Preferred stock also must be structured carefully to assure that the conversion premium (the difference between the price of the preferred and the price of the common) is reasonable at the time the shares are issued.

Some companies have faced a problem when they issue dividend-paying stock to employees and find that under state laws they must pay the same dividends to holders of this stock outside the plan. This problem can be remedied, however, by changing the non-ESOP shares into some kind of non-dividend paying security beforehand.

The Rules of the Loan

A loan to an ESOP must meet several requirements. The loan must be at a reasonable interest rate, and only the stock in the ESOP acquired with the proceeds of the loan can be used as collateral (although the company or seller can, and almost invariably does, make its own guarantee with the lender). Only the dividends of the shares in the plan (called distributions in S corporations), contributions from the employer to repay the loan, and earnings from other investments in the trust contributed by the employer can be used to repay the loan. This means that dividends paid on shares acquired by the ESOP outside of the loan cannot be used to repay the loan, nor can the ESOP normally sell off shares in the trust to repay the loan unless the plan is terminated or the company is sold. In that case, all unpaid-for shares can be sold to repay the loan, with any amounts remaining after the sale being allocated to employees.

The loan must be without recourse to the ESOP, and must be for a specified term. The interest rate can be variable or fixed. There is no limit on the term of the loan to the company other than what lenders will accept (normally 5 to 10 years). Because the loan is usually made to the company and then reloaned to the ESOP, however, these bank-imposed limits do not necessarily limit the term of the company-to-ESOP loan. Provided the company can show that extending the term benefits employees, the term of the company-to-ESOP loan can be longer. For instance, extending the term of the loan to fit within the annual contribution limits would clearly benefit employees because, without such an extension, the plan would be disqualified. Extending the term to keep benefit levels more constant over a longer term might also qualify provided the benefit levels are significant.

Shares in the plan must be held in a suspense account. As the loan is repaid, these shares are released to the accounts of plan participants. The release must follow one of two formulas. The simplest is that the percentage of shares released equals the percentage of principal paid, either that year or during whatever shorter repayment period is used. In these cases, however, the release cannot be slower than what normal amortization schedules would provide for a 10-year loan with level payments of principal and interest. The principal-only method usually has the effect of releasing fewer shares to participants in the early years.

Alternatively, the company can release shares based on the percentage remaining in the account based on principal and interest paid. To do this the company divides the principal and interest payment it makes by the sum of (1) the principal and interest it still needs to pay and (2) the principal and interest it paid already that year. Stated more simply, the company bases its release on the total amount of principal and interest it pays rather than on the amount of the principal it repays. ESOP loans with a term of over 10 years must use this principal-plus-interest approach.

In either case, it is important to remember that the dollar value of the shares released each year is rarely the same as the amount contributed to repay the loan. If the price of the shares goes up, the amount allocated will be higher, in dollar terms, than the amount contributed; if they go down, the dollar value of the amount released will be lower. The amount *contributed to repay principal* is what counts for determining whether the company is within the limits for contributions allowed each year.

Refinancing ESOP Loans

Companies can refinance an existing non-ESOP loan with an ESOP loan under the same rules as if the loan were a new one. If a loan is refinanced, the shares are still allocated based on their original purchase price. Companies can refinance a loan that is reloaned to an ESOP without restriction because that transaction is between the company and the lender. ESOP loans themselves can also be refinanced under limited circumstances. Generally, a company wants to extend the existing term of the loan. In some cases, this is done because the company's payroll has shrunk, and the existing term requires payments that are above the contribution limits. In other cases, the company needs to repay the loan more slowly because of cash flow problems. The Department of Labor (DOL) has approved such refinancings. However, some companies want to refinance because their stock value has risen quickly, and they believe they are delivering "too much" value to employees. The DOL is much less favorable toward these refinancings.

Buying Back Unallocated Shares

Shares that have not yet been paid for are held in suspense before being allocated when loan payments are made. Some companies want to buy these shares back from the ESOP, often because they see them as a good value or because managers want to own more shares. In general, regulatory bodies frown on this because it denies employees an implied future benefit. Such repurchases are approved only in unusual circumstances. Note that this scenario is different from an outside purchase of all ESOP shares. That can be done if the ESOP trustee deems the sale to be in the best interests of plan participants.

Limitations on Contributions

Contributions to the Plan as a Whole

Congress was generous in providing tax benefits for ESOPs, but there are limits. Under Code Section 404, a C or an S corporation can contribute and deduct up to 25% of the total eligible payroll of plan participants to cover the principal portion of the loan, plus contributions to pay interest on the loan. In C corporations, contributions to fund the interest payments on the debt do not count toward the 25%-of-pay limit, but in S corporations they do.

Eligible pay is currently defined as pay not exceeding $255,000 per year (as of 2013; this figure is indexed annually for inflation, rounding in $5,000 increments). Note that eligible pay only includes people actually in the plan. In many "Section 1042" transactions, sellers, 25% shareholders, and certain relatives of these individuals are not included in the plan, nor are most new employees and others not yet eligible to participate.

In addition, dividends paid on shares acquired by the ESOP loan in a C corporation can be used to repay the loan, and these are not included in the 25%-of-pay calculations. Dividends used to repay a loan must release additional shares (from the suspense account if there are enough; from other corporate shares if not) to employee accounts with a value equal to the dividends. If employees leave the company before they have a fully vested right to their shares, their forfeitures, which are allocated to everyone else, are not counted in the percentage limitations. Theoretically, total payments made to the ESOP to repay a loan do not have to be adjusted downward because of other benefit contributions, but limits on how much individuals can get usually make this irrelevant. Employee deferrals to a 401(k) plan now count as eligible pay.

IRS private letter rulings have clarified that in C corporations (but not in S corporations), the 25% limit for deductible contributions to repay principal is *in addition* to contributions to other defined contribution plans, rather than being combined with them.[1]

Annual Allocations to the Accounts of Individual Participants

In evaluating limitations on contributions, it is important to understand that in addition to the deductible contribution limits based on the total amount of pay of plan participants as described above, there are limits under Code Section 415 on the amounts that can be allocated to any individual account in a given year (called the "annual addition" limits).

First, no one ESOP participant's account can receive more than 100% of pay in any year from principal payments on the loan, or more than $51,000 (as of 2013; this figure is adjusted annually for inflation in $1,000 increments), whichever is less. Contributions that do not meet these limits are forfeited and reallocated to other plan participants.

Second, the limits include company contributions to other defined contribution plans. Employee contributions to benefit plans are also counted toward this 100% of pay or $51,000 (as of 2013) figure.

Third, the interest is excludable from the annual addition limits for C corporations only if not more than one-third of the benefits are allocated to highly compensated employees, as defined by Code Section 414(q). If the one-third rule is not met, forfeitures are also counted in determining how much an employee is getting each year. In S corporations, interest always counts. Once an ESOP loan is repaid, forfeitures must count toward the annual addition limits.

In calculating the annual addition limits for a leveraged ESOP that is repaying a loan, the dollar amount of the contributions used to repay the loan is generally counted as the annual addition, not the actual value of the shares that are released from the suspense account to a participant's account. For example, if the value of the company's stock has increased since the ESOP transaction, a $50,000 allocation to a participant's account will be used by the ESOP to repay the loan and release shares worth more than $50,000 into the participant's account.[2]

---

1. See, e.g., PLR 200732028 (2007).

2. Alternatively, the plan may provide that the lesser of (1) the contributions used to repay the loan or (2) the actual value of the shares is used. Treas. Reg. § 1.415(c)-1(f)(2)(ii).

The effect of these provisions is that companies must very carefully assess just how much they can afford to borrow through the ESOP. Plans that violate these rules can suffer severe penalties, including plan disqualification. If payroll is inadequate, however, companies do have alternatives. The initial loan can be for less than the amount optimally desired, with a successor loan paying the rest. It may be possible to negotiate a longer loan period in order to stretch out contributions. Finally, and most importantly, companies can use dividends to repay the loan.

Using Dividends to Repay the Loan

C corporations (but not S corporations) can take a tax deduction when using dividend payments to repay the ESOP loan. These payments are not included in any of the calculations described above. Dividends on both allocated and unallocated shares are normally used to repay the loan. The dividends must be "reasonable." While this term has never been defined, most consultants believe it is a percentage of share value consistent with what other companies in the industry would pay given similar levels of profits. The dividends also must not be so high as to provide employees with "unreasonably" high compensation. The payment of excessive dividends will cause the dividends to be taxed, although it is not certain whether only the excess dividends or the entire dividend will be taxed. In extreme cases, the plan can be disqualified. Nonetheless, some very profitable companies can use dividends to increase the percentage of pay going to an ESOP to 50% or more.

Many companies use preferred stock in their ESOPs to allow for higher dividend payments. Whatever kind of stock is used, the amount of the dividends must be allocated to employee accounts. Companies normally allocate these amounts in the form of shares released from the suspense account. For dividends paid on allocated shares and used to repay the loan, the value of the shares released must be at least equal to the amount of dividends used. That means that allocations of these shares to employees will be equal to the ratio of their account balance to the prior total amount in the plan. Dividends on unallocated shares that are used to repay the loan can be allocated on this same basis, on the basis of relative compensation, or according to some more equal formula. The allocation must occur in the year the dividend is used to repay the loan.

Using Distributions in S Corporations to Repay the Loan

Most non-ESOP S corporations make distributions of part of their earnings, usually to help owners pay their taxes. In an ESOP-owned S corporation, distributions received by the ESOP on both allocated and unallocated shares can be used to repay the ESOP loan (as well as for other purposes, including to repurchase shares or simply add diversity to employee accounts). Distributions paid on unallocated shares can release shares from the suspense account based on either the company's normal allocation formula (often a percentage of eligible pay), or based on the relative percentage of shares already allocated to a participant's account. For shares that have already been allocated from the suspense account, the distributions must release shares from the suspense account based on relative account balances.

Other Issues

The rules for leveraged ESOPs are similar to the rules of other qualified plans in terms of participation, allocation, vesting, and distribution, but several special considerations apply.

Who Must Be Included

All employees over 21 who work for more than 1,000 hours in a plan year must be included in the plan unless they are covered by a collective bargaining unit, are in a separate line of business of at least 50 employees not covered by the ESOP, or fall into one of several anti-discrimination exemptions not commonly used by leveraged ESOPs. If there is a union, the company must bargain in good faith with it over inclusion in the plan if the union wants to discuss the issue. Companies may want to include union employees in leveraged plans to maximize the amount of eligible payroll. If the ESOP does not replace other benefits, this normally can be done without requiring a reopening of the contract.

Allocations to Employee Accounts

As shares are released from the suspense account, they are allocated to individual employee accounts. This allocation can be on the basis of relative compensation (generally, all W-2 compensation is counted), but a more equal formula can also be used, such as per capita or seniority, or some combination. These other formulas must be written in such a way, however, that no highly compensated individual gets more than would be allocated under a relative pay formula.

If a more level formula is used, note that a formula that serves as an allocation cap (such as ignoring pay over $80,000 per year when allocating by relative compensation) can effectively reduce the level of eligible payroll. The company can only make deductible contributions that it can allocate, so if it cannot allocate as much due to a formula that caps allocations at a certain level, it cannot contribute as much. In some cases, this may mean there is insufficient eligible payroll to amortize the loan through the ESOP.

Vesting Rules

The allocated shares are subject to vesting. Employees must be 100% vested after three years of service (cliff vesting), or the company can use a graduated vesting schedule not slower than 20% after two years and 20% per year more until 100% is reached after six years. If the ESOP contribution is designated as a match to employee 401(k) deferrals (whether the ESOP and 401(k) are integrated or not), and the match is used to meet the "safe harbor" anti-discrimination rules for 401(k) plans, the contributions must vest immediately. Generally, if a company contributes 3% or more to the accounts of all eligible 401(k) participants (whether they make deferrals or not) or matches at a rate of at least 100% for the first 3% of pay employees defer, and 50% for the next 2%, then it does not have to test for participation in the 401(k) plan.

Diversification

When employees reach age 55 and have 10 years of participation in the plan, the company must either give them the option of diversifying 25% of their account balances among at least three other investment alternatives or must simply pay the amount out to the employees. This option extends for each of the next four years. The diversification limit applies to the total share value in the participant's account (not the total account balance, part of which may already be diversified). If a participant chooses to diversify part or all of the eligible 25% in any year, an additional amount in each subsequent year can be diversified so that the total amount of shares diversified is 25%. Thus, an employee could diversify 25% of subsequent stock allocations, but could not diversify 25% of the total allocations in year one, then 25% of what is left in the account year two, etc. (this incorrect approach would result in over 75% diversification in year five). In the sixth year, eligible employees can increase their diversification to 50%.

Distribution Rules

Under the rules governing ESOPs, when employees retire, die, or are disabled, the company must distribute their vested shares to them not later than the last day of the plan year following the year of their departure. For employees leaving before reaching retirement age, distribution must begin not later than the last day of the sixth plan year following their year of separation from service. Payments can be in substantially equal installments over five years or in a lump sum. In the installment method, a company normally pays out a portion of the stock from the trust each year. The value of the stock may go up or down over that time, of course. In a lump-sum distribution, the company buys the shares at their current value but can make the purchase in installments over five years as long as it provides adequate security and reasonable interest. If a distribution is over $1,035,000 (as of 2013), the five-year period can be extended by one year for each additional $205,000 (as of 2013), up to five additional years (these amounts are indexed yearly). Distributions are generally made in stock or cash, but the participant has the right to demand shares. ESOP shares must be valued at least annually by an independent outside appraiser unless the shares are publicly traded.

There are two important exceptions to these requirements. If a company's charter or bylaws state that all or substantially all of the company's stock must be held by employees (inside or outside the ESOP), or the company is an S corporation, the company can require the employees to take the cash value of the stock. Second, C corporation leveraged ESOPs can delay the start of repayment until the loan is repaid, although exceptionally long delays (typically over 10 years) to start distributions are not recommended by ESOP advisors because they can make repurchase obligations unmanageable and damage employee morale. Note that the law does not specifically provide that S corporations can also delay payment until after a loan is repaid. Advisors generally agree that this was a technical oversight in the law and that the IRS would not object to a plan document including this provision (and we have no indication that they have yet done so).

The delayed distribution rules apply only to the shares acquired by the loan, not to all shares in the plan. For employees who terminate before death, retirement, or disability, the rules are relatively straightforward. Distributions do not have to start until the plan year following the plan year in which the loan is repaid. Distribution must be completed in the plan year following the plan year in which the loan is repaid or, if later, the date distribution would have to be completed under the normal distribution rules specified in the plan document and/or distribution policy. If a participant leaves in 2011, for instance, and the loan is repaid in 2013, the participant could still have to wait until 2017 to get a distribution, provided the plan and/or distribution policy provides that distributions do not have to start until five plan years after the end of the plan year the participant terminates.

There are also general qualified plan rules that apply to all aspects of distributions from retirement plans, including ESOPs, that can trump these ESOP-specific rules. Generally, the ESOP-specific rules will be the ones that are relevant, but the general rules state that distribution must start no later than the 60th day after the end of the plan year in which the later of these events occur: (1) the participant reaches age 65 or, if earlier, the plan's normal retirement age; (2) the 10th anniversary of participation in the plan; or (3) termination of service. These provisions can create somewhat complex interactions, as when an employee quits before retirement and after 10 years of service, and shortly thereafter reaches retirement age; at that point the general rules require distributions to begin, instead of waiting for the sixth plan year after the employee quits under the ESOP rules.

As with all retirement plans, distributions for any more-than-5% owners must begin no later than April 1 following the calendar year in which a participant reaches age 70½, and distributions for other employees must begin no later than April 1 following the later of (1) the calendar year in which the participant reaches age 70½ and (2) the calendar year in which the participant retires.

Finally, private companies and some thinly traded public companies must repurchase the shares from departing employees at their fair market value, as determined by the appraiser. This so-called "put option" can be exercised by the employee in one of two 60-day periods, one starting when the employee receives the distribution and the second period one year after that. The employee can choose which one to use. This obligation should be considered at the outset of the ESOP process and factored into the company's ability to repay the loan.

Within these limits, as long as a company does not discriminate between employees, it can set its own distribution requirements. A commonly recommended best practice is to write the maximum allowable distribution schedules into the plan but provide that a written distribution policy may provide more flexibility on a non-discriminatory basis (the NCEO has model distribution policies in the issue brief *ESOP Distribution Policies*).

Voting Rules

Voting is one of the most controversial and least understood of ESOP issues. The trustee of the ESOP actually votes the ESOP shares. The question is "who directs the trustee?" The trustee can make the decision independently, although that is very rare. Alternatively, management, the board, or the ESOP administrative committee can direct the trustee, or the trustee can follow employee directions.

In private companies, employees must be able to direct the trustee as to the voting of shares *allocated* to their accounts on several key issues, including closing, sale, liquidation, recapitalization, and other issues having to do with the basic structure of the company. These general rules may differ in how they apply to specific cases, however. In public companies, employees must be able to vote on all issues. Private companies have the option of passing through voting rights on a one-person, one-vote basis.

Voting rights are more complicated than they seem, however. First, voting is not the same as tendering shares. So while employees may be required to vote on all issues, they may have no say about whether shares are tendered. In public companies, this is a major issue. Almost all public companies now write their plans to give employees the right to direct the tendering, as well as voting, of their shares, for reasons explained below.

Second, employees need not be given the right to direct the voting of unallocated shares. In a leveraged ESOP, this means that for the first several years of the loan, the trustee can vote the majority of the shares, if that is what the company wants to do. The company could provide that unallocated shares, as well as any allocated shares for which the trustee has not received instructions, should be voted or tendered in proportion to the allocated shares for which directions were received.

Third, if employees vote their shares on all issues, a company can still restrict their voting rights. The major issue on which employees would vote, of course, is who sits on the board of directors. A company could amend its bylaws to restrict who can be nominated for the board, thus retaining control within a management group, if desired.

The concern with voting rights may be more smoke than fire, however. Research by the NCEO indicates that employees are very conservative shareholders who normally support existing management. In a recent Gallup poll, 56% to 71% of people surveyed said if they were employee owners, they would prefer to let management make decisions on a variety of corporate issues. Managers of companies that are employee-owned and employee-controlled say that employee voting rights have made very little difference in how their companies actually run. Of course, there are always exceptions, and these can cause legitimate management concern.

Unlike private companies, public companies usually want employees to direct the voting and tendering of shares. That is because trustees in an ESOP may see their role as maximizing the share value of the plan's holdings, thus causing them to accept an offer by an unwanted suitor. Employees, however, will probably (but not always) vote against a raider. In a key court decision, a Delaware judge ruled that if employees can independently direct the voting and tendering of the shares, an ESOP may be an effective defense against a takeover. There are many other considerations here, however.

Military Leave

In the case of employees on military leave, employers must comply with the Uniformed Services Employment and Reemployment Rights

Act (USERRA). By law, for all retirement plan benefits, employees must continue to receive vesting as if they still worked for the company. There is no break in service. Employers are not required to make contributions or allocate forfeitures during the time of service, however. If there is a 401(k) plan, the employee has the right, over the lesser of five years or three times the length of employment, to make make-up contributions, and the employer would have to match these according to the formula that otherwise would have applied.

Accounting and Reporting Issues

Accounting for ESOPs is covered elsewhere in this book, but the basics can be outlined here.

The debt acquired by the ESOP must be counted as corporate debt, even if the corporation is able to get the loan without guaranteeing it. Until the late 1980s, banks often could obtain unguaranteed loans for their ESOPs and use the ESOP purchase of their shares to increase their capital, but this is no longer an acceptable accounting practice.

The offsetting debit to the liability recorded by the employer should show up as a reduction in shareholder equity (it appears as a contra equity account). The argument here is that the shares in the ESOP are held by a third party but are not yet paid for. As the loan is repaid and shares are released, both the liability and the offsetting contra equity account are reduced.

Amounts contributed or committed to be contributed to the ESOP need to be reported, with contributions to cover principal charged to compensation expense and interest accounted for as it normally would be allocated. Shares held by the ESOP are deemed as outstanding for calculations of earnings per share. For plans started after January 1, 1993, the value of shares released is their current market value. Plans started before then can use the acquisition cost or market value. Dividends should be charged to retained earnings except when dividends are used to repay a loan. Then they are charged to retained earnings for allocated shares and current earnings for unallocated shares. Where the principal-only method of repaying the loan is used, it may be necessary to take a charge to earnings equivalent to what the principal and interest method would produce.

These guidelines are based on the position of the American Institute of Certified Public Accountants (AICPA). Most were adopted by the Financial Accounting Standards Board in 1989. They are not laws or regulations, but standard accepted practices. Some accountants differ on one or more of these points.

Issues for S Corporations

Since January 1, 1998, S corporations have been able to have an ESOP own stock in the company. ESOPs are exempted from the unrelated business income tax (UBIT) that other non-taxable owners of S corporation shares are required to pay on their share on corporate profits. In other words, whatever percentage of the company the ESOP owns would not be subject to any current taxation. On the other hand, S corporation ESOPs do not have the same tax benefits available to C corporation ESOPs. Specifically, (1) owners of S corporation stock cannot use the tax-deferred Section 1042 rollover when selling to an ESOP, (2) dividends (i.e., S corporation "distributions") used to repay a loan or passed through to participants are not deductible, and (3) interest payments on an ESOP loan count toward the contribution limits.

There are complex rules to prevent abuses of the non-taxability of an S corporation ESOP's ownership interest. The good news for the large majority of S corporation ESOPs is that this will not affect them in any way. It will, however, prevent ESOPs from being used in S corporations to benefit just a few usually highly paid people. Specifically, the law defines certain ESOP participants as "disqualified persons." These are individuals who own 10% or more of the shares in the ESOP, counting allocated shares, their pro-rata share of unallocated shares, and, outside the ESOP, any stock options or other synthetic equity (this includes, among other things, a variety of kinds of deferred compensation). Direct ownership does not count. They also include people who, using family attribution rules, own 20% or more of the shares this way. If these individuals collectively own 50% or more of the company, including their ownership of synthetic equity, direct ownership, and ESOP ownership, then there is a 50% excise tax on the company, and allocations and account accruals to the disqualified individual are taxed as ordinary income. "Accruals" in this case means additions to plan participant accounts or to anyone who is a disqualified person under the rule even if he or she is not a plan participant. Accruals include additions to accounts from any source, not just allocations from company contributions. For instance, if unvested shares are reallocated within the plan, that would count as an accrual, as would additional shares bought within the plan from cash distributions. Violations can also occur if the number of shares changes. In short, anything that brings the disqualified persons over 50% ownership triggers the draconian taxes the law entails.

Another consideration for S corporation ESOPs concerns the payment of distributions. If the company makes distributions to any shareholders, it must make pro-rata distributions to the ESOP as well. So if a $1 million distribution is made in an S corporation 30% owned by its ESOP, the ESOP gets $300,000. This money can be used to repay a loan or just be added to employee accounts to create a cash balance in the plan that can be used to buy back shares in the future or for other purposes. While this can be very beneficial for S corporations with ESOPs (this is money that would have otherwise been used to pay taxes that now can be used for other purposes), as ESOP ownership percentages grow, the distribution amounts can be extremely large, creating in the process equally large employee accounts and, in some cases, violations of ESOP rules stating that the assets must be primarily held in employer securities. It also means that those with shares get richer and richer, while new employees get far less.

It is common for S corporations to convert to C status before setting up an ESOP so that sellers can take advantage of the Section 1042 rules that allow the deferral of gains on sales to qualifying ESOPs. S corporations doing that cannot reconvert to S status for five years. It is even more common for C corporations to convert to S status when they become 100% ESOP-owned. This conversion almost always makes financial sense, but there are some issues that need to be considered:

1. If a company uses LIFO (last in, first out) accounting procedures, there is an immediate recapture over four years of any excess inventory (not assets) with LIFO over what would have been the case with FIFO (first in, first out).

2. Built-in gains are taxable when assets are sold in C corporations. When they convert to S status, any gains on property sold within 10 years of conversion are taxable as income.

3. If a company has passive investment income for more than 25% of its income, then after conversion there may be an additional tax in excess of this. If income stays at this level for three consecutive years, then the company would lose its S status.

4. Certain tax benefits of being a C corporation, such as net operating losses, capital loss carryovers, and minimum tax credit from the AMT, cannot be carried over after electing S status.

5. S companies can only have one class of stock.

6. Interest payments count in calculating the contribution limits for the ESOP. Forfeitures of unvested shares that are reallocated also count toward the ESOP individual annual account addition limits.

7. Very small companies (less than 15 employees) may have a very hard time meeting the S corporation anti-abuse tests even if they have very standard or even egalitarian approaches to allocations.

8. In some cases, the ESOP deductions will be large enough so that the C corporation effectively has little or no tax anyway.

Valuation Issues

A separate chapter in this book deals with valuation concerns, but a few should be noted here. The fact of leveraging the ESOP may decrease the value of the shares because of the new debt, but not necessarily on a dollar-for-dollar basis. Valuation involves more issues than just the book value of the company, and these may provide additional value even after a 100% buyout. Although the company would have no net asset value after such a transaction, it still would have the capacity to earn income, and this provides some level of value. Second, the valuation should reflect the ongoing repurchase obligation. If it does not, then the shares will be overpriced; the obligation is a legal one and a very real liability to the company.

Freezing or Terminating an ESOP

Each year, 3% to 4% of all ESOPs are terminated; an unknown percentage are frozen, usually because the sponsor wants to create a different kind of benefit plan, wants to recapture some of the ESOP's ownership, or, more rarely, has financial problems. Terminating or freezing a plan is a decision that can be made by the plan sponsor, but, in both cases, there are special considerations that need to be taken into account.

Freezing an ESOP

In a frozen plan, further contributions to the plan stop, but the plan continues to operate. Employees receive their distributions according to the rules of the plan document. Theoretically, the plan could continue until the last participant receives a distribution. As in all ESOP matters, the ESOP committee or other fiduciary should be careful to document and justify all decisions.

At first blush, it may seem that freezing the plan is the simplest step when a company wants to wind down its ESOP. There are, however, a number of problems freezing can create. First, the plan must still be administered, with annual reports to participants and the government. In closely held companies, there must be an annual valuation. Top-heavy rules (i.e., rules imposed on plans in which highly compensated employees' accounts exceed 60% of the total employee accounts) must still be met. Remaining participants still get to partake in any stock appreciation. Any improprieties in the plan could lead to lawsuits. These additional costs and risks may more than offset the benefits from not simply terminating the plan and paying people out, as discussed below.

Terminating an ESOP

When a plan is terminated, all participants become fully vested, and distributions must begin within a year of the plan's termination. Payouts for the distributions can be made in equal installments with adequate security over five years (or more in cases of distributions over $1,035,000, as of 2013; this figure is indexed each year). Alternatively, the amounts can be rolled over into a successor plan, such as a 401(k) or profit sharing plan. The company could make the rollover mandatory, or it could give employees an option. Participants must have the right to receive their distribution in stock if they so choose unless the plan calls for cash distributions and all or substantially all the company's stock is owned by employees.

In a nonleveraged plan or a leveraged plan where the loan is fully repaid, the amounts that are allocated are paid out directly to participants or rolled over into a successor plan. Terminating a leveraged plan where the loan has not yet been repaid is more complicated. To repay the loan, the company must reacquire the shares or sell them to another buyer. If the shares are not at a price that repays the remaining amount, the company makes up the difference; if selling the shares results in more cash than is needed, a more complicated situation arises. An amount equal to the basis paid for the shares divided by the proceeds of the sale, multiplied by the excess after the loan is paid off, must be allocated to employee accounts on the basis of their relative share balances. In other words, any windfall from the shares goes to employee accounts.

Terminating or freezing a plan is not a decision to be taken lightly. There are important fiduciary issues to consider that should be discussed carefully with qualified counsel.

Should You Undertake a Leveraged ESOP?

Obviously, leveraged ESOPs are complicated and carry many obligations and restrictions. Their benefits are also substantial, however. So how does a company decide whether an ESOP is worthwhile, or, given that, whether a leveraged or nonleveraged ESOP would be more advantageous?

Before deciding on a leveraged ESOP, it is worth considering a nonleveraged ESOP. Some companies may not have the ability to obtain or repay a loan, or they may simply be averse to debt. In other cases, the company may not want to be constrained by a debt repayment schedule, instead preferring to make periodic discretionary cash or stock contributions to the ESOP. This means shares will be bought out more slowly, but if they are bought from existing owners, this may be acceptable if the owners are not in any rush to sell or think the stock price will rise over time.

A primary reason for using leverage is to enable the ESOP to acquire enough stock (30% of the company) to qualify sellers for the tax deferral of Section 1042. Some companies do this by accumulating cash contributions in the ESOP until there is enough to meet this goal (as noted above, this generally can be done for a few years), or putting in some cash, then borrowing the rest.

If an ESOP is used to borrow money, several issues need to be considered. First, companies need to consider any dilution effects the ESOP may create if the company is issuing new stock to the plan, rather than buying back existing shares. Most ESOPs do not issue new shares, however.

Second, companies need to evaluate carefully what the tax benefits of the plan will be (remember that all these benefits have no value to unprofitable corporations) and whether they will have adequate cash flow to service the debt. This may seem obvious, but in several cases, leveraged ESOPs have been used to buy out an owner, leaving the employees with more debt than they could handle, and their companies have closed.

Third, alternative forms of financing should be considered. The long-term benefits of an ESOP are hotly debated by experts solely concerned with their corporate financial impact. Equity or even straight debt may be preferable in some cases. That is especially the case when companies seriously consider (as too many do not) the repurchase obligation. ESOPs have up-front cash flow benefits, but require a long-term liability.

Fourth, public companies must consider the impact of the ESOP on shareholder relations. Leveraged ESOPs can make their financial reports look worse, unless offset by changes in other benefit plans. Yet these changes may have an undesired impact on employee morale.

Fifth, the size of the payroll relative to the size of the ESOP must be considered. ESOPs may simply not work in some companies because their total compensation is too small. While some companies may expect growth to solve the problem, lenders may take a more skeptical look at just how likely growth really is. For some companies, the answer to this may be a nonleveraged ESOP. This allows much greater flexibility in determining when and if to make contributions. The company can contribute as little or as much as it wants within applicable limits, however. This means, of course, that shares will be acquired more gradually, rather than bought all at once with a loan repaid over several years.

Finally, in any ESOP, but especially in one where the financial commitment is as fixed as a leveraged plan, ESOPs should never be installed solely because their tax benefits look appealing. Unless managers and owners are comfortable with and committed to the concept of employee ownership, an ESOP is not a good choice. Other financing and benefit plans offer tax breaks of their own. What ESOPs do is allow companies to share ownership with employees at the same time that they are financing other corporate objectives. But if a company is concerned only with the latter issue, and regrets the requirement of the former, eventually the ESOP will be seen as a mistake. ESOPs work best when companies share information, communicate about the plan regularly, and get employee owners more involved in the day-to-day decisions affecting their work. Absent these efforts, an ESOP is just another benefit plan and may not be the best one for any of the parties involved.

Chapter 2

Understanding ESOP Valuation

Outside Valuation's the law [handwritten]

Corey Rosen

Why Do You Need a Valuation?

There is a T-shirt in the Exploratorium museum in San Francisco with a picture of Albert Einstein in a policeman's hat. The legend on the T-shirt says "186,000 miles per second. It's not just a good idea, it's the law." If you want to have an ESOP in a closely held company, an independent, outside valuation is not just a good idea, it's the law. You must have an appraiser figure out what a willing buyer would pay a willing seller, assuming both have all the relevant information they need to make the transaction.

Book value usually under-estimates [handwritten]

Many people ask us at the NCEO why they can't just use book value or some other formula instead of having an appraisal done. But book value usually understates the real worth of ownership. Most businesses are worth some multiple of their earnings, earnings that are generated not just by assets, but by such intangibles as reputation, expertise, contacts, innovative ideas and processes, etc. On the other hand, other owners tell us they know that in their industry, businesses sell for an average of x times earnings or some other multiple. But your business is not likely to be average. If in using a formula you come up with a value that is just a few percentage points higher or lower than a more accurate assessment of your company's value, the costs will be much greater than the cost of a valuation.

How Often Must an Appraisal Be Performed?

The law requires appraisals to be done at least annually, but there may be circumstances that require a more frequent appraisal. The law

appraisal must be at least annual [handwritten]

FMV @ time of transaction

also requires that ESOP transactions be conducted at the current fair market value. That means that any time the ESOP buys or sells stock, it should, in theory, be based on a fair market valuation as of the date of the transaction.

IRS prefers valuation opinion letter

If the ESOP is buying shares from an owner or the company, for instance, it should try to time its purchase to coincide with the most recent appraisal as closely as possible. The IRS prefers that the transaction be accompanied by a valuation opinion letter stating that the valuation is effective as of that date. On an ongoing basis, in an ideal scenario all transactions related to plan distributions (such as a departing employee selling shares back to the company or the plan) occur at a specific annual date that is timed as closely as possible with the annual appraisal. In practice, what this usually means is that the appraiser provides a report on a regular schedule and the plan administrator closes the plan year as soon as possible after that. Statements are then mailed to employees, and transactions are completed during a short window following the closing. Plans can also be written, however, to say that the value will be as of the last valuation, even if that is as much as one year old.

But what happens if there has been a significant change between the time of the transaction and the appraisal? Unfortunately, there is no specific guidance on this. Say, for instance, that an appraisal is completed as of April 1 ("as of" here means that the price set in the report is effective that date, not that the report is completed that date). By the fall, there has been a significant change up or down in company prospects. Is the April 1 appraisal acceptable? If the ESOP is buying shares from the owner and the transaction has been delayed since the appraisal report, a new report is probably required. If the company or ESOP is buying back shares from the participants, if the plan clearly states that the most recent appraisal will be used, and this practice is followed consistently, then this should be acceptable. But in some cases the trustee or company leadership may be concerned that significant changes need to be dealt with. For instance, a likely large drop in share price since the last appraisal would mean the company would have to buy back shares at a high price just at the time its cash flows are under pressure. Conversely, a significant increase in price could leave some departing employees feeling cheated—and more likely to sue. Companies concerned about these possibilities would need plan language stating "bring-down" letter

that the distribution would occur as of the most recent appraisal if the trustee believes there have not been major changes in share price during that time, but that a new appraisal could be requested if there is reason to believe major changes have occurred. To support that, a trustee might ask for a "bring-down" letter from the appraiser to indicate whether the value is still appropriate. Your ESOP advisors should be looked to for guidance on these issues any time there is any doubt.

Who Performs an Appraisal?

no precise definition of independent

The law requires an independent, outside appraisal from someone who is customarily in the business of doing business appraisals. There has never been a precise definition of what "independent" is, however. Clearly, some people are excluded—your board, your attorney, your brother-in-law, your CFO, your CPA, or anyone else with a direct financial relationship with the company. But what about your CPA firm (but not the person doing your books), or the valuation advisor who is affiliated with your attorney? Many people argue that if your CPA firm is large and can establish a "firewall" separating its audit and valuation sections, then that is acceptable. Others contend that even this is risky. Similarly, some people say you can use firms affiliated with your advisers (such as a valuation firm that pays a fee to your attorney for referrals), but most experts would argue that is not a wise policy.

We suggest

We strongly suggest that you pick a firm that has no other business relationship with your company than the appraisal itself. A high percentage of lawsuits involving ESOPs concern valuation. The law looks primarily to process, not results, in determining whether the appraisal was fair to the ESOP. An appraisal done by a truly independent, qualified firm establishes a degree of credibility not possible any other way. With any other firm, there is always the possibility that the appraisal was done with an eye toward getting or keeping the company's business for the other parts of the firm or the affiliated parties involved in other parts of the transaction. The costs will rarely be lower in using someone not truly independent, so it is best to err on the side of caution.

competence

The other major issue in determining whether an appraiser is qualified is competence. Here there are two areas to evaluate. The first is general business appraisal competence. Anyone can be a business appraiser.

anyone can be a business appraiser

high % of ESOP suits involve valuation

Trade organizations

No specific degree or licensing procedure is required by states or other entities. The appraisal industry does try to be self-regulating, however.

There are a number of organizations, offering a wide variety of designations, that provide some kind of business appraisal certification. Among these are the American Society of Appraisers (ASA), the National Association of Certified Valuation Analysts (NACVA), the Institute of Business Appraisers (IBA), and the American Institute of Certified Public Accountants (AICPA). Each organization provides some kind of technical education program providing certification designations. There are so many designations now that they can become quite confusing. It is worth asking an appraiser what designations he or she has and what was required to obtain them, but making comparisons on designations alone may be difficult.

In addition to these qualifications, you should also look at experience, in-house training requirements for the firm, whether the appraiser has spoken or published on the subject, and, of course, references.

Business appraisal competence is not enough, however. As will become clear later, there are many ESOP-specific issues. These issues can have a dramatic impact on the final valuation. Your appraiser should be able to demonstrate specific experience and expertise in ESOPs. Ask for a list of ESOP clients and call them. Find out whether the appraiser belongs to the relevant professional organizations (the NCEO and the ESOP Association), regularly attends professional conferences on the subject, and has spoken or written on ESOP-specific issues. If the appraiser claims to have ESOP expertise but does not meet these criteria, look elsewhere.

How Do You Find a Good Appraiser?

Both the NCEO and the ESOP Association maintain lists of appraisers and other ESOP professionals that are available to members. Neither group endorses the people listed in the guides, but at least this provides assurance that the appraisers are involved in the relevant professional organizations. Most active ESOP appraisers will appear on both lists. Your other professional advisors usually will also have recommendations, and you should ask other ESOP companies whom they have used.

One issue to decide is whether to pick an appraiser from a large or small firm. Large firms typically have an appraisal reviewed by one or more other staff members and may have additional credibility should there be a legal challenge. Some small firms, however, have excellent reputations and also may provide for internal reviews. Generally, large firms charge more, but this is not always the case. While there is not a right or wrong answer here, size per se is probably not a critical issue when comparing firms of comparable price, competence, and compatibility.

In picking an appraiser, it is wise to interview at least two or three candidates. You will find that there are significant variations in price, experience, and appraisal philosophy. The first two are obvious things to look for, but the third may seem a little confusing. Why ask about philosophy?

Different ESOP appraisers have different approaches to key appraisal issues, such as discounts for lack of control or liquidity (these are discussed below), or in their general appraisal approach (such as whether they rely more on earnings multiples or on comparable companies). These will have a potentially dramatic effect on value. Initial assumptions tend to get locked into your ongoing ESOP appraisal. It will always arouse suspicion if, a few years after the first ESOP appraisal, you decide you are unhappy with the approach and choose someone else who comes in with a different set of assumptions. Your business won't have changed, but ESOP participants and the IRS may now see a very different appraisal number. At best, you have a serious communications problem; at worst, you have a lawsuit or problem with the government.

Similarly, it is both expensive and risky to decide after the initial appraisal that you do not like the result and ask to have a second appraisal from someone else. The appearance, at least, is that you are shopping for an appraisal advantageous to you, not accepting an objective report. To head off such complications, the ESOP trustee or the person who will become the trustee (as we shall see, the appraiser works for the trustee) should interview appraisers beforehand. If the ESOP trustee decides down the road that the appraisal is in some way potentially faulty, the best approach is to hire a third party to do a review of the appraisal report (but not redo the appraisal). This is fairly inexpensive. If the review is positive, then things can continue; if not, the trustee may seek some changes in approaches by the appraiser or decide to hire an alternative firm (but not the one doing the diagnostic).

Some appraisers, as well as some legal advisors, may tell you that this too makes it appear you are shopping the appraisal. But we would argue, along with most of the ESOP legal community, that without these discussions the trustee cannot make an informed decision on who is best to do the appraisal.

Now, however, comes the tricky part. These interviews must be designed to find out what approaches are going to be in the best long-term interest of the ESOP and its participants. The goal is not to find the appraiser who will come up with the highest price. Instead, the trustee should be looking to assure, as best as possible, that the appraisal will support the long-term viability of the plan and that the appraisal will use methodologies that are generally accepted by the appraisal community and the regulatory authorities. That means the price will not be so high as to endanger the company's ability to pay for it nor so low that the current sellers will not want to sell. The appraisal assumptions and procedures must also assure that future participant distributions will be at their proper value. The ultimate price must fit within the range of what reasonable appraisers could agree is not more than fair market value.

Admittedly, these are somewhat vague guidelines, but ESOP appraisal is an art, not a science. While the process cannot be exact, however, it can and must be informed. A careful discussion with the appraiser about these issues prior to engagement can avoid confusion and unhappiness down the line. Note, however, that the appraiser may (appropriately) say that an initial discussion does not provide enough information to make an assessment of which approaches will work best.

Who Hires the Appraiser?

The appraiser's client, by law, is the ESOP trust, no matter who actually writes the checks to cover the fees. This has important implications. First, the letter of engagement should clearly specify that the appraiser is working for the ESOP. Second, it means the appraiser is not trying to find the highest price that can be justified or, as in some tax-oriented appraisals, the lowest. Third, it should remind everyone involved that the point of the appraisal is to protect the interests of the ESOP participants by ensuring the ESOP does not pay more than fair market value in any purchase from an outside seller and that employees are paid fair market value for company shares in their ESOP accounts.

appraisal sets maximum price, but not minimum price

Is the Appraised Price the One the ESOP Pays?

Once the appraiser has provided a report saying what fair market value is, that is not the end of the story. Many people incorrectly assume that this is the price that the ESOP must pay. Instead, the law requires that the ESOP cannot pay *more* than this price when purchasing shares from a seller. Indeed, it is the responsibility of the ESOP trustee to negotiate the best price possible, which sometimes will be less than the appraised value.

This negotiation might take a number of tacks. In a few cases, the seller prefers to sell for a lower price, usually because of concerns about the ability of the ESOP to repay the loan or just because the owner wants to be generous. In others, the trustee argues that tax benefits to a seller to an ESOP should come partly back to the ESOP in the form of a lower price. It is the ESOP, after all, that justifies the lower price as a result of its tax advantages. In still other cases, the ESOP trustee is simply bargaining for a better deal and, given the lack of other options the seller may have, is able to exert some leverage.

These scenarios all envision using an ESOP to buy shares from an existing owner. Sometimes an ESOP acquires new shares, such as when it borrows money to purchase shares to help finance growth, or when it accepts contributions of shares. In these cases, the trustee has less negotiating leverage because the contributions to the ESOP are diluting other owners, not buying their shares. Still, the size of a loan might be such that a lower price is needed to fit within legal requirements, or owners may wish to add another bargain element for the ESOP.

Gift tax in theory if pay too little

Theoretically, a sale at a price far below fair market value could trigger a gift tax for the ESOP (which would then pay unrelated business income tax). In practice, we have never seen this become an issue. There is enough leeway in how shares are valued so that by varying assumptions this problem can almost always be overcome.

What Does the Appraiser Need from You?

In preparing an appraisal report, the appraiser will need a lot of data from you. The more precise and well prepared these data are, the better (and possibly cheaper) the appraisal will be. The following list indicates the key items appraisers generally need, although there may be other things requested:

- Financial statements, typically for the last five to ten years, preferably audited (but many smaller companies will present only reviewed statements). Income statements, balance sheets, cash flow and capital statements, and any explanatory footnotes or other material are included.

- Budgets or projections

- List of subsidiaries, if any

- Leases and contracts

- Compensation schedules

- Prior appraisals

- Dividend history and expectations

- Legal documents

- Prior sales or offers

- Shareholder list

- ESOP documents

- Operational information, such as sales by customer, patents, departmental budgets, competitors, etc.

In addition to a review of these documents, the appraiser will want to interview management and possibly board members, suppliers, customers, advisors, or anyone else deemed to have critical information. One or more site visits will be arranged. During these interviews, any significant issues that could materially affect operations, such as a pending environmental liability, a new competitor, management changes, or a patent expiration, for instance, should be thoroughly discussed.

What Is in the Appraisal Report?

Valuation reports can run from several pages to hundreds of pages, depending on the complexity of the company and the terms of the engagement. The report will cover several issues. The basis for the appraisal of the company as an enterprise should be thoroughly explained and justified (for instance, if the appraiser chose to use an earnings ratio as a key element, why that was more appropriate in this case than some other methodology). Then there should be a discussion of any discounts or premiums applied to that value for the shares the ESOP is purchasing. Again, a thorough explanation of assumptions and rationale should appear. The data used for making the determination should be outlined, and any weightings or judgments used in assessing these data should be elaborated. Any special factors that affect valuation findings, such as a change in management that could reduce future value, should be covered. Reports usually also include a number of charts and tables showing different indications of value based on different methods. *U.S.DO.L.*

In addition to these matters, the report should follow the guidelines *regs* included in the U.S. Department of Labor's proposed regulations concerning valuation. Among other things, these include a discussion of the business, its markets, and general economic considerations affecting value. The company's book value should be considered, along with any goodwill or other intangible assets and the company's dividend-paying history and capacity. The price of similar companies, if any, should be provided. Finally, issues relating to marketability and control concerns need to be reviewed.

The final valuation will be a blending of these issues. Because there is no formula for valuations, however, each report will be different.

Steps in the Valuation Process: What Is Fair Market Value and How Is It Calculated?

In calculating how much the ESOP can pay, the first step is to determine how much the business is worth as an entity. There are three basic approaches used to determine this: the asset approach, the market approach, and the income approach.

three approaches

Asset Approach — *least used*

This is the simplest approach and one many closely held companies already use to value their shares for purchases by key employees. It is also the least used method in ESOP appraisals. In this approach, a company is assessed based on either the liquidation value of its assets or its adjusted book value. The adjusted net asset methodology approach takes the balance sheet and transforms it from an accounting document to an economic one. For instance, an asset may be fully depreciated on the balance sheet, but still have resale value on the market. Liabilities may not appear on the balance sheet because they are contingent, such as a possible environmental issue (cleaning up a landfill, for instance). Inventories also need to be adjusted for what they could currently sell for in the market. Any accounts receivable and payable not on the balance sheet need to be considered. Any intangible, but marketable, assets (such as a trade name) need to be assessed.

While these methods are simple, they are also usually wrong. People usually want to buy a business because it can yield them a return on their investment; the ESOP always looks at a purchase this way. While a company's assets are part of what creates an income stream in a company, they are only part of it. All sorts of other factors—expertise, reputation, contacts, processes, labor practices, and other issues—condition how much a company can make. The asset approach has even less relevance when only a minority stake is being sold because minority owners cannot force a liquidation of assets. *less relevance w/a minority stake*

Market Approach

The next approach is to see what, if any, evidence there is of how much people would pay for stock in the company or comparable companies. There may be, for instance, a history of stock sales in the company, or there could be other valid offers. These offers, however, do not necessarily establish a value that the ESOP can pay.

First, the offers may have been for control when the ESOP is not buying control (or vice-versa). Stock is worth more when it is part of a control purchase, as discussed more fully below. Second, the offer may have come from another company with a synergistic interest in the target company. If International MegaCompany can gain operating efficiencies, or eliminate competition, by buying Pete's Pizza Parlors, it will pay more for Pete's than would a buyer who could not capture these efficiencies. The ESOP is always a *financial* buyer; it must be able to justify its purchase based on the return that investment yields as a stand-alone company, although heavy acquisition activity in a given industry may influence market pricing upward and should be considered. Third,

ESOP is always a financial buyer

the offer or sale may have been for less than market value, as often is the case with sales to managers based on book value. These and similar concerns make this methodology useful in providing benchmarks, but far from determinative.

A related methodology is to look at comparable companies. The ideal comparison is another closely held company in the same industry with similar financials. But these ideal companies are hard to find, and, even if found, there are usually no data of any kind on transactions, much less the detailed data to allow apples-to-apples comparisons (such as whether the sale was to a synergistic buyer). Private companies do not have to report such data to any public source, but some valuation companies have access to databases that track sales that their firm has followed.

Better data are available from public companies, but here several complicating issues arise. First, many public companies have multiple lines of business. Second, they are almost always larger, and often much larger, than the company being appraised. Third, they may have very different capital structures than closely held companies. These and other differences make direct comparisons difficult. Most business appraisers are experienced in dealing with these complications, however, so the data on stock prices in these companies can yield useful insights about the typical ratios (such as share price to annual earnings) that can be applied, with appropriate adjustments, to provide benchmarks for applying multiples to the company being valued. When using public companies, the indicated value for the company being appraised is a minority interest, freely marketable value because the share prices of the publicly traded companies represent small minority interests in the public company.

Another source of market data is comparable companies (including closely held companies) that have been merged and/or acquired. Multiples paid in such comparable transactions are generally applied, with appropriate adjustments, to the subject company's earnings and cash flow. Because the multiples based on these data are calculated using prices paid for entire companies, the indicated value for the subject company is a value for the entire company (enterprise or control value). It may or may not indicate a "liquid" value, depending on whether or not the comparable merged and/or acquired companies were public or privately held at the time of acquisition.

However a market approach is constructed, a company's earnings will be "normalized" to reflect how another buyer would operate the business. This is discussed in more detail below in the section on the income approach to valuation.

Income Approach

A third set of methodologies falls under the income approach. The basic theory behind these methodologies is that a buyer is looking to make a reasonable return on an investment over an acceptable period of time, given the relative risk of the investment. A theoretical willing buyer is looking at a variety of investment choices. There are safe ones with low returns (CDs, T-bills, etc.), somewhat riskier ones with higher returns (stocks and bonds), and still riskier ones with the highest returns (individual companies). It has to be this way: the higher the risk, the greater the return an investor will demand. In buying a company, then, the investor needs to know two basic things: what the risk is and what the income flow is that will result from the investment. There are a number of ways to conceptualize these factors, but the two most common are referred to as capitalization of free cash flow and discounted cash flow.

Capitalization of free cash flow method: With the capitalization of free cash flow (FCF) method, the appraiser develops an estimate of the company's sustainable level of free cash flow. This is usually based on history and estimates of what future FCF will be. FCF is defined as follows:

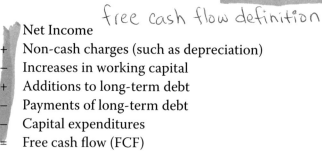

free cash flow definition

Net Income
+ Non-cash charges (such as depreciation)
− Increases in working capital
+ Additions to long-term debt
− Payments of long-term debt
− Capital expenditures
= Free cash flow (FCF)

Free cash flow is normally used because that is the basis from which an investor can earn a return from the investment either in the form of dividends or investment of the FCF back into the business for future growth. However, some appraisers prefer other variations on the future income theme, such as earnings before interest, taxes, and depreciation.

After these numbers are determined, they are adjusted to reflect nonrecurring items and special considerations. For instance, there may have been a large one-time expense that lowered earnings (and thus FCF) in a prior year, or an anticipated one-time expense in the future projections. Very commonly the pay and perquisites of executives or other employees need to be adjusted to reflect what the market rates for these individuals are, unless these practices will remain in place after the transaction. If the CEO is making $400,000 a year and has a company-paid vacation to France every year, the appraiser might determine that these expenses would be substantially reduced if someone else bought the company. This excess is added back to earnings if the levels of compensation will not continue into the future. Similar adjustments to earnings and cash flow are typically made before applying multiples in the market approaches as well. After analyzing historical and potential earnings, the appraiser will determine a single figure called "representative earnings."

Finally, a capitalization rate is applied to these representative cash flows. The concept here involves some complex math, but the basic idea is simple. The appraiser is trying to determine what the present value of a future stream of sustainable FCF is. The rate is derived by subtracting the expected long-run rate of FCF growth from the company's discount rate. The discount rate, in turn, reflects the rate of available risk-free investments and the risk adjustments appropriate for the fact that this is an equity investment made in a company of a certain size (there is less risk in a large company) with specific risk concerns.

For instance, an appraiser might determine that in a particular business, the expected FCF growth rate is 6% per year. The discount rate is 25%. The capitalization rate is now 19%, and this is divided into expected FCF to determine the company's value. If the next year's (or sustainable) FCF is $3 million, the company would be worth $3 million divided by .19, or $15.8 million before considering appropriate discounts or premiums. The underlying concept here is that the investor is looking to obtain a return on investment that justifies the risk. In this case, the return would be 19% on the expected annual FCF.

Discounted cash flow approach: A similar approach is the discounted cash flow method. Here the discount rate (25% in this case) is applied to a measure of FCF. Theoretically, all the earnings could be paid out this way to justify the investment, and this would provide a benchmark for determining value. Again, annualized free cash flows are determined; these are then discounted back to the present at the required rate of return or discount rate. The appraiser will add a terminal value at the end of the forecast period to complete the analysis.

In both methods, attention must be paid to the special tax benefits the ESOP provides the company as these can change expected earnings and cash flow.

What Discounts or Premiums Apply to ESOP Value?

Whether or not any discounts and/or premiums apply to the indicated values derived using the valuation methods described above depends on numerous factors. In ESOP valuations, discounts generally fall into two categories: liquidity and control. These are discussed in more detail below. But before knowing whether to apply a discount, it first must be determined whether or not the valuation is being conducted on a controlling interest (or enterprise) basis or a minority interest basis. Then, depending on the method and data used within the valuation method, appropriate discounts and/or premiums are applied. Similarly, whether to apply a liquidity discount depends on whether the comparisons used to determine value are based on liquid or illiquid interests in companies.

By way of example, assume that the valuation assignment is to determine the enterprise (controlling interest) value of a company and that the appraiser has used market approaches and an income approach. In the market approach, the appraiser used two subsets of information, comparable publicly traded companies and comparable companies that had been merged and/or acquired.

As noted earlier, the value indicated based on comparable publicly traded companies is a minority interest, freely traded (or completely liquid) value. Therefore, in order to arrive at a value for an entire enterprise, it would generally be appropriate to apply a premium for control and a discount for lack of marketability. Conversely, if the valuation assignment were to value the company on a minority interest basis,

[margin note: discounts: liquidity & control]

it would not be appropriate to apply a minority interest discount to the comparable publicly traded approach, because the value indicated already reflects a minority interest discount. It would, however, be appropriate to consider a discount for lack of marketability.

The value indicated from the comparable merged and/or acquired company approach represents an indication of control or enterprise value. Thus, if the subject company is being appraised on a controlling interest basis, then it is not appropriate to apply a control premium to this approach. That would be a double discount because the value is already reflective of controlling interest value since the multiples used in this approach are based on prices paid for entire companies. On the other hand, if the subject company is being valued on a minority interest basis, then it would be appropriate to apply a minority interest discount to this approach. Whether or not a discount for lack of marketability is appropriate using this approach generally depends on if the comparable merged or acquired companies were public at the time of the acquisitions.

The income approach may indicate either a control or minority interest value. Generally speaking, if control level free cash flows were used, the income approach indicates a control value. If minority interest level free cash flows were used, the income approach generally indicates a minority interest value. However, variations in the discount rate and/or free cash flows used may result in some sort of blended indication of value, the subject of which is beyond the scope of this chapter.

The critical element to understand with regard to whether or not discounts and/or premiums are appropriate is that it *depends on the base from which the premiums and/or discounts are proposed.* If discounts are needed, they generally fall into two categories below: liquidity and control.

Liquidity and Repurchase Obligation Issues

If you buy shares in IBM, you can sell them any time and get your money in three days. If you buy stock in Sally's Computers, there is no ready market for the shares. You might not be able to sell them for years, and you may have to settle for less than market price if you need the money and no one is eager to buy. This lack of marketability creates a discount *closely held co. discount*

over the price for the sale of otherwise comparable shares in a public company or shares in a closely held company about to be sold (because in this case there is immediate liquidity). So in any closely held company selling shares other than in a total sale, there is a discount over what the price would be for publicly traded shares, usually in the range of 20% to 40% depending on the circumstances, such as any restrictions on the sale of stock, buy-sell agreements, prospects of an initial public offering, dividends, or the availability of other buyers.

Many ESOP appraisers contend that the presence of the ESOP mitigates or even eliminates this discount. ESOP rules require that departing employees have the right to put their shares back to the company (or have the company fund the ESOP to do this) at fair market value. This seems to eliminate the lack of marketability.

The reality is more complicated, however. First, there must be some assurance that the company can really muster the cash to repurchase the shares. Second, the put option does not belong to the ESOP, for whom the appraisal is being made, but the participants in the plan. Third, the put option applies only in a limited window of time and only when people leave the company or can diversify their accounts. That is hardly the equivalent to owning shares in a public company.

Appraisers argue back and forth on the legal and practical issues involved here. The typical discount for lack of marketability in an ESOP company, according to NCEO studies, is 5% to 15%. A higher discount may discourage the seller from selling; one that is too low saddles the ESOP with an obligation on an ongoing basis to buy shares at a price that reflects an aggressive assumption about value (because these assumptions normally have to be carried forward).

In most appraisals, the liquidity discount is where the repurchase obligation is reflected. In that case, setting a liquidity discount should not simply consist of picking some round number that seems reasonable. The obligation of a company sponsoring an ESOP to buy back shares from departed ESOP participants represents a future use of nonproductive assets. This obligation means money is not available for other uses. If the company "recycles" the shares, either by contributing cash to the ESOP to buy the stock or by buying the stock directly and recontributing it to the ESOP immediately or over time, then the number of outstanding shares remains the same, while the discounted future cash flow per share declines by the magnitude of the obligation. This should produce an iterative set of calculations. The obligation will lower value, but the new lower value means a lower future obligation. The calculations keep being repeated until a solution is found. The resulting number should be a precise one, just as other elements of the valuation are, not just a "best guess."

On the other hand, if the company redeems shares and does not recontribute them, then the number of shares drops proportionately to the decreased future cash flow, producing a neutral effect on share value but reducing enterprise value.

An emerging (and we think better) practice for the repurchase obligation, however, is to calculate the amount of the obligation over the coming years that is in excess of what the company would normally pay for benefits. This results in lower projected earnings. That results in a lower value, which makes the repurchase smaller, so the calculation is run again (and again and again in what is called an iterative process) until a solution is found. This calculation is affected by how much cash is in the ESOP, recycling versus redemption policies, and other factors.

Including the repurchase obligation in the valuation requires the appraiser to have a copy of a repurchase analysis. Companies that do not go through this process, and do not require the appraiser to factor it into the final result, will overpay for the shares, endangering the future ability of the company to grow or to honor its repurchase obligation.

Lack of Control (Minority Interest) Discounts and Control Premiums

The second major issue is control. When someone buys a controlling interest in a company, a premium is paid. This is why share values soar in takeover battles. If the ESOP is buying less than control, it pays less per share (a "minority interest") than would a buyer of controlling interest. Studies of control premiums in public company transactions are compiled every year. These typically are in the 30% range, but can vary widely. Again, however, note that it is only appropriate to apply a minority interest discount to a value indication that represents control.

The first source of variation in control premiums is the company's specific situation. In some companies, a 33% stake may carry some

apply minority interest discount ONLY when value represents control

limited control rights; in others, even a 51% stake may not convey full control rights. There might be specific shareholder agreements that limit control of any owner, such as a buy-sell agreement, covenants with banks, or contractual obligations. These and other issues make control a more complex concept than "control" or "no control"; there are shadings in between as well.

A second source of variation is what the ESOP will buy in the future. If the ESOP starts at a minority stake but has a right to buy enough to get control in the future, can it pay a control price? Is the seller obliged to sell to the ESOP? Many advisors say yes, provided that the option allows the purchase in not more than three to five years and gives the ESOP trustee control rights even before gaining a numerical controlling interest. Some appraisers take a tougher view, some a more liberal one. Some appraisers even argue that if the ESOP is buying less than 51% in any purchase, it pays a non-control price (for instance, if the ESOP owns 51% and buys another 20%, it would pay a non-control price for this 20%). There are no right or wrong answers, although in all things related to valuation, we would urge a cautious approach.

Note, however, that the decision on whether to pay a control price is not one the appraiser makes. It is the trustee's decision. The appraiser can provide advice on this issue, but the trustee must decide whether the ESOP really has the attributes and rights necessary to allow a control price to be paid. *trustee decides whether to pay a control price*

The Impact of Leverage on Valuation

If the ESOP borrows money, it will have an impact on valuation. The interest expense on the new debt the company now has taken on to fund the ESOP will show up on the balance sheet and, in any event, represents a significant non-productive expense. While this generally will not reduce value dollar-for-dollar (there are ESOP tax benefits, the company may grow, and there is a discount for the future value of money), it will reduce the post-transaction value. This effect will disappear as the loan is repaid.

This impact is important for two reasons. First, employees need to understand why this drop occurs. Their own account values start at the lower value and thus are not reduced by the debt (unless the loan is to a previously existing plan), but they need to understand the issue to avoid communications problems. Other owners will also see their share price drop, of course. If they plan to sell before the ESOP loan is repaid, this could present a problem. In some cases, companies arrange for pro-rata sales from owners to avoid this issue.

Another potential issue is where the ESOP is one of a group of purchasers. Say an ESOP is borrowing $6 million, four managers are contributing a total of $2 million based on a loan to be repaid out of future payroll deductions, and private investors are contributing $2 million in cash in a $10 million transaction. Should the share allocation be 60%/20%/20%? The private investors will likely argue that because their investment carries more risk (the ESOP loan is non-recourse to participants, and the managers won't be paying anything if the company fails and they are not getting paid), they should be able to get a higher allocation of shares than either group. The managers might argue that their risk level falls in between but that they deserve a higher allocation than the ESOP.

In the 1980s, this became a very contentious issue as ESOPs were used in some very large leveraged buyouts. In some cases, the ESOP was allocated only the capitalized value of its tax benefits. The Department of Labor and the courts did not favor this approach, saying it meant the ESOP was paying more than fair market value. Since then, advisors have recommended a variety of alternatives, such as giving investors warrants in addition to their shares, selling some investors preferred shares, structuring part of outside investments as higher-interest paying debt, and so on. In other cases, everyone just accepts the straight allocation. If you are in a situation such as this, it is critical to get experienced advice.

A more common issue is what happens when the company does a second-stage or other subsequent ESOP transaction involving leverage. Say that Oxy Industries has a 30% ESOP that has been fully paid for. Now it takes out a loan to buy another 30% of the shares. The price of the shares in the ESOP will probably go down because of the leverage, at least for a while. On the other hand, participants will probably be getting a higher contribution each year to pay for the new shares. But some participants will leave (or will have already left and will be waiting for a distribution) and see their share value drop. They may well get paid out before the debt is repaid, so the leverage effect may still be there. Some companies simply say this is the luck of the draw. Others have some kind of price protection for employees who could be affected. Most commonly (and most safely) this would be the company making an additional cash payment to employees in this situation to make up the difference between the price at the time the leverage occurred and the current price, if lower. Some other structures have been used or proposed as well, but they are beyond the scope of this chapter.

In contrast, what happens if the company or the ESOP takes on debt for other purposes, such as making an acquisition, buying new capital, or refinancing existing debt? If the acquisitions are for a fair price or better, this will not affect value and could even raise it. If debt is refinanced at a lower rate, that too could raise future appraisals. The key here is that debt for these kinds of purposes would rarely be an issue of concern for the ESOP fiduciary.

S Corp ESOP – no FIT on Scorp earnings

S Corporation ESOP Issues

S corporations with ESOPs have a tremendous tax advantage. When the ESOP trustee receives a statement of the pro-rata share of earnings on which taxes would be paid each year, the trustee can ignore it. ESOPs do not have to pay federal tax on their share of the S corporation's earnings. This is usually true for state taxes as well. Hence, with a 100% ESOP-owned S corporation, there is no federal (or usually state) income tax to be funded. Clearly, having an ESOP in an S corporation can enhance earnings, yet, just as clearly, a potential willing buyer would be unlikely to maintain the ESOP. So from that buyer's standpoint, the future earnings would be unaffected by this special tax benefit. As a result, the standard practice in ESOPs is not to "tax-effect" the earnings. However, over time, the tax savings will help the company grow faster and more profitably.

Conclusion

The requirement to have an ESOP appraisal is designed to assure that the ESOP process is fair to all parties involved. While many business owners would prefer to set their own prices using a formula or a number derived from prior offers, these simplistic approaches rarely result in the price the ESOP would pay as a financial buyer. ESOP trustees, as well as owners, managers, and employees of ESOP companies, need to understand the valuation process well.

Chapter 3

Accounting for ESOP Transactions

Rebecca J. Miller

dramatic impact

Too frequently, the accountant is called into the picture after a leveraged employee stock ownership plan (ESOP) transaction has been implemented and the financing obtained. To start educating the plan sponsor on the accounting treatment of leveraged ESOPs at that late date is likely to be an unhappy experience. By that time, the transaction may be too far down the road to be able to avoid or minimize any potentially adverse accounting treatment. Many people simply do not recognize the dramatic impact that a leveraged ESOP will have on the financial statements of the plan sponsor.

The purpose of this chapter is to describe the basics of accounting for leveraged ESOP transactions so that potential plan sponsors and their advisors can anticipate the accounting presentation and structure the transaction where possible to minimize any complications created by the accounting. This chapter is only a primer on the rules covering the accounting for leveraged ESOPs and will not cover all of the intricacies of very sophisticated ESOP applications. Nor will it go into much detail on the accounting for nonleveraged ESOPs.[1] ESOP sponsors or potential sponsors will still need to get their accounting firms involved in the early stages of planning because the sophisticated equity structures of many ESOP transactions create equally sophisticated financial reporting consequences beyond what is covered in this brief overview.

---

1. This chapter does not cover nonleveraged ESOPs because the financial reporting for them is substantially similar to that for profit-sharing plans. Sponsors of nonleveraged ESOPs should, however, pay attention to the footnote requirements discussed later in this chapter because those requirements apply to all ESOPs, leveraged or not.

Background

Before describing the accounting rules in detail, it may help readers who are not accountants to understand how these rules are created. Most people have some understanding of how tax and Employee Retirement Income Security Act of 1974 (ERISA) regulations are written. If questioned on the accounting rules, however, those same people would have little idea of how an accounting principle is developed and what importance it has to their financial future.

Even after the Sarbanes-Oxley legislation, the accounting profession remains a self-regulated professional group. In an attempt to achieve uniformity, the profession establishes Generally Accepted Accounting Principles (GAAP). Most accounting standards are issued by the Financial Accounting Standards Board (FASB). FASB issues Statements of Financial Accounting Standards, referred to as FASB Statements, and FASB Interpretations, referred to simply as Interpretations. Before 2002, the next level of accounting authority was issued by the Accounting Standards Executive Committee (AcSEC) of the American Institute of Certified Public Accountants (AICPA). This group issued Statements of Position, referred to as "SOPs." An SOP does not depart from the general rules established by the FASB. Since 2002, AcSEC has only issued guidance on industry-specific accounting and auditing matters. In 2009, AcSEC was renamed as the Financial Reporting Executive Committee or FinREC. The last group authorized to issue accounting authority is the Emerging Issues Task Force (EITF) of the FASB. This group is the least formal and is authorized only to interpret current standards. Such interpretations, however, do have the standing of GAAP. These interpretations are referred to as EITF Issues.

The FASB provides for a public comment period before it releases a statement. When comments are received, the staff reviews them. Changes may be proposed in response to such comments. In any event, any standard passes in front of the applicable board or boards before final approval. If the public comments raise serious issues that result in major modifications in a proposal, a second comment period may be provided before finalizing a standard.

A FASB Interpretation can be released without any public comment but generally involves significant time in drafting. The EITF, on

Financial Accounting Standards Codification

the other hand, can respond quite quickly. It holds approximately 10 meetings every year. If consensus can be reached at a single meeting, new GAAP may be created.

In 2009, all U.S. GAAP in whatever form (FASB, SOP, EITF, etc.) was combined into a single document. This is the Financial Accounting Standards Codification (ASC), referred to below as the "Codification." Practitioners are gradually becoming familiar with this structure. To the person unfamiliar with U.S. accounting standards, this may be very helpful, as all literature on a specific topic is covered by a single section of the Codification. The user no longer has to search through the FASBs, SOPs, EITF Consensus Opinions, FASB Staff Interpretations, etc., to ascertain the governing provisions on that topic.

Besides these private entities, the SEC issues accounting pronouncements for public companies. These releases typically concern issues relevant to the public market. However, if there is no other GAAP pronouncement on the topic, an SEC Accounting Release may be considered to apply even to private companies. In addition, the SEC substantially influences GAAP through its participation with the FASB. These releases are, however, separate documents and are not found in the Codification.

SEC Accounting Release

It is rare for any other entities to become involved in drafting accounting rules for the public. Within regulated industries, the regulatory agencies may require deviations from GAAP or may supplement GAAP. However, the regulatory rules are applied only in preparing statements for the regulators, not for other users who request GAAP statements.

Today, the accounting standard setters are dealing with the concept of "convergence." As more and more businesses compete in a global marketplace, the need for uniform standards across nations has become evident. To address this concept, the accounting community formed the International Accounting Standards Board (IASB). U.S. GAAP has been evolving in conjunction with the international standards. Where common principles exist, common standards are developed. However, U.S. GAAP continues to have a separate application to most ESOP sponsors.

Most users of financial statements (lenders, for example) will require that a "clean" opinion be provided by the auditor. A clean opinion is one that states that the financial statements have been subject to generally accepted auditing standards and are presented in accordance with gen-

clean opinion

erally accepted accounting principles with no exceptions. The failure to provide a clean opinion may reduce the amount of credence that the users will have for the statements. Because most leveraged ESOPs do involve a lender, it is important to understand how the ESOP will affect the financial statements of the plan sponsor.

It is possible to receive a "clean" opinion on financial statements that are prepared based upon an "other comprehensive basis of accounting." This might be, for example, cash basis, modified cash basis, or income tax basis. Commercial lenders typically require GAAP-basis financial statements, so the remainder of this chapter focuses on that manner of presentation.

Specific ESOP Accounting Authority

From 1976 until 1989, the accounting for ESOP transactions was controlled by Statement of Position 76-3, "Accounting Practices for Certain Employee Stock Ownership Plans," published by the AICPA in 1976. This was issued before the Internal Revenue Service (IRS) and the Department of Labor (DOL) had finalized their regulations governing the operation of leveraged ESOPs. This statement, referred to as SOP 76-3, was later affirmed as GAAP by Statement of Financial Accounting Standard No. 32.

At the time that SOP 76-3 was issued, because ESOPs were quite new, most of them were very simple arrangements. All of the later activity involving convertible preferred stock, debt service with deductible dividends, reduced interest loans, immediate allocation loans, and so on was not yet encouraged through special tax incentives. Therefore, most of the plans were straightforward financing and compensation devices.

In response to this, a simple accounting standard was developed. The upsurge in ESOP activity during the 1980s, however, highlighted inadequacies in the SOP. This caused a great deal of activity on the part of the FASB's Emerging Issues Task Force during 1989 to amplify and apply the terms of the SOP to the creative ESOP applications that came about because of the 1984 and 1986 tax law changes. In 1989 the EITF dealt with only 20 accounting issues, four of which were ESOP-related.

This flurry of activity caused the accounting community to rethink the existing ESOP guidance. In fall 1989, the AcSEC formed a committee to address ESOP accounting. After more than three years of meetings, public comments, and hearings, a revised model for the reporting of leveraged and non-leveraged ESOPs was approved. That standard applies to shares acquired on or after December 31, 1992. A plan sponsor may elect to apply it to earlier periods, but is not required to do so. The prior accounting rules under SOP 76-3 and the numerous EITF consensus opinions may continue to be applied.

Apart from this development, a significant controversy took place during 1991 and 1992 as a result of a proposed revision of Statement of Financial Accounting Standards No. 96 (SFAS 96) dealing with the reporting of income taxes. A portion of the changes in SFAS 96 also has a significant impact on sponsors of ESOPs. The revised statement, SFAS 109, effective for 1993 with no transition rule, interacts with the new ESOP accounting standard in critical ways for sponsors that use dividends for debt service.

In addition, in the spring of 1992 the EITF issued a clarification on the treatment of the tax benefit on common shares held by an ESOP for reporting earnings per share. This is EITF Consensus Opinion 92-3. This opinion was necessary to integrate the impact of SFAS 109 and prior EITF Consensus Opinion 90-4. (Note that Consensus Opinion 90-4 applied only to preferred dividends. The impact of the tax benefit of common dividends was specifically not the subject of consensus.)

All of the ESOP accounting authority that developed during this period can now be found in the Codification at ASC 718-40. Since some users of this text may have access to the original SOP, all references from this point forward in this chapter will be to both documents. The history refers only to the original pronouncements because there was no Codification at that time. For those needing to identify where the historical pronouncements fall into the Codification, the FASB has provided a cross-referencing tool.

The remainder of this chapter covers how a leveraged ESOP affects the plan sponsor's financial statements. The reader is cautioned to pay specific attention to the structure of the loan discussed in each paragraph. In the 21st century, it is as common for the ESOP to borrow funds indirectly through the plan sponsor as it is for the ESOP to borrow directly from a lender or with seller financing. The financial reporting by the plan sponsor is substantially similar in each case, but the entries required to record the plan's activity will vary. The following discussion is for financial statement purposes only and does not bear on the income tax treatment of ESOPs.

To best understand the financial reporting of leveraged ESOPs, the reader should think of the transaction as being substantially similar to a treasury stock acquisition. If a company purchased shares from a current shareholder with debt, the company's financial statements would record the debt and a negative entry to equity referred to as "Treasury Stock." If the company subsequently rewarded those shares to other employees as compensation, the fair market value of the shares would be recorded as compensation on the award date, treasury stock would be reduced by the original cost of those shares, and additional paid-in capital would be adjusted for the difference. This is only a simplified view of the results, but it sets an easily recognized framework in which to understand the accounting for a leveraged ESOP transaction.

Balance Sheet

The first financial statement presented in any official set of financial statements is the balance sheet. Generally, this has three parts: assets, liabilities, and equity. For sponsors of certain ESOPs another section, temporary equity or mezzanine capital, also may be present. That is classified on the debt/equity side of the balance sheet between long-term debt and equity.

Assets

Other than the obvious increase in cash or other assets resulting from the financing aspect of certain plan structures, an ESOP has no direct effect on the asset side of the balance sheet. The assets of the plan are not reported as assets of the sponsor. In the event that the sponsor has a note receivable from the plan because internal financing was used, that note receivable is not recorded as an asset; instead, it affects the equity section.

Liabilities

For purposes of this discussion, it is important to recognize the kind of debt an ESOP might incur. Typically, the debt is the original stock acquisition loan. The ESOP may have directly borrowed funds from a commercial lender. However, seller financing is also considered a direct loan. Also, if the ESOP distributes shares to a plan participant and then repurchases those shares with a note, that is a stock acquisition note subject to these accounting standards. Where the ESOP borrows funds from the plan sponsor, it is an indirect or two-step loan. The ESOP accounting does not change with respect to the structure of the financing obtained by the plan sponsor to fund that loan.

Under ASC 718-40/SOP 93-6, all ESOP debt is reflected on the financial statement of the plan sponsor. There is no potential for off balance sheet financing under the current standards. This is based upon the fact that the ESOP has no ability to repay this debt except for funds provided by the plan sponsor through contributions or dividend/S corporation distribution payments on the shares held by the ESOP.

One major, unanswered question remains after nearly 20 years have passed: How is the debt to be reflected upon the balance sheet of a subsidiary that participates in a single plan that covers the parent corporation and some or all of the subsidiaries? In the minutes from the June 19, 1989, EITF meeting, there is a specific reference to the fact that the EITF members did not discuss this matter. There is nothing specific in the Codification regarding this. Common sense would argue that if the subsidiary's employees are covered by the plan, then that subsidiary is, theoretically, benefiting from that portion of the ESOP and obligated to fund its portion of the ESOP debt. Thus, such subsidiary should reflect that portion of its debt.

In any event, the accounting practitioner might initially argue that it makes no difference since GAAP requires a consolidated balance sheet in the case of a parent/subsidiary group. In this case, it is irrelevant where the debt is initially recorded—the parent or the subsidiary—since it all ends up in the same place. A problem arises in the case of separate financial statements of regulated enterprises (banks or savings and loan institutions, bonded warehouses, etc.) that are subsidiaries of holding companies. In these cases, the regulators or bonding companies frequently impose rigid financial ratio or other reporting requirements. These requirements affect the way the enterprise can conduct its business. Generally, however, the regulators seem to look at GAAP financial statements of the operating subsidiaries only. They may not look at any debt of the holding company when analyzing the subsidiary's ability to do business. In the past, these entities have used leveraged ESOPs at the parent company level. This has left the debt at that level and not brought it down to the operating subsidiaries. To date, disparity remains in accounting practice on whether to "push down" this debt from the parent to one or more of the subsidiaries. As discussed under ASC 718-40/SOP 93-6, the argument against "push-down" accounting has been weakened for post-1992 transactions. If the debt is recorded by the employer because it is the source of future debt service and the employees are all at the subsidiary level, it makes sense that the subsidiary is the entity that will be servicing the debt and recording the debt. The only recommendation that can be made at this time is to discuss the matter specifically with your accountant in the event that any recording of the debt at the subsidiary level could have an adverse effect on the plan sponsor's ability to do business. This issue, however, has had less attention paid over recent years due to the dominance of indirect or two-step loans rather than direct loans.

All of this discussion under "liabilities" has focused on the major issue of the recording of the ESOP loan by the sponsor. There is also an ancillary, though occasionally equally frustrating, issue. This is the recording of the current accrual for the current year's contribution to the plan. Generally, any long-term obligation will be separated annually into two pieces. These are the short-term piece, the amount that is payable in the next 12 months, and the long-term piece, the amount not payable within 12 months. The first is recorded as a current liability. The second is recorded as a long-term liability.

In most cases, where the employer makes its qualified plan contribution after the end of the year, the balance sheet will show a current liability for any accrued plan contribution. If a sponsor has a leveraged ESOP with outside debt, the unfunded amount of the "accrued contribution" that is applicable to future debt service will already be recorded in current liabilities in the form of the current portion of the ESOP debt. Until the contribution/payment is actually made, that debt cannot be eliminated. If the current accrual for the contribution that is intended to make this payment is also recorded, that portion of current debt will be reflected twice in the current liabilities section of the plan sponsor's balance sheet. This double-counting of this obligation is avoided by the expense recognition methodology under ASC 718-40/SOP 93-6. No accrued contribution is recorded except for contributions that are *not* to be applied to debt service in the current period.

The above section covers the recording of a direct loan to the ESOP. In the more typical two-step or indirect loan transaction, the company borrows funds from another source and makes a second loan to the ESOP. Occasionally, the sponsor has the funds on hand and makes a direct loan to the ESOP. In such cases, the credit relationship between the ESOP and the sponsor is not recorded as an asset or a liability. Not only is the long-term debtor/creditor relationship not reflected, but there is also no payable to the ESOP for the accrued contribution or receivable from the ESOP for its requirement to return these funds to the sponsor for that year's payment. Obviously, to the extent the sponsor borrowed funds from another party to finance this event, that loan would be recorded, and any other accrued contribution to the ESOP to fund distributions or cover plan expenses would also be recorded.

Equity

Anyone who has had an introductory accounting course will remember that every credit entry must have an equal debit entry or the books will not balance. In booking the ESOP loan for a direct loan or the transfer of cash to the plan for an indirect loan, a credit is recorded. As stated earlier, the establishment of the ESOP has no impact on assets, where debits would normally show up on the balance sheet. That leaves us with only one other place to put this dangling debit: the equity section. At the same time that the debt is recorded or the cash is advanced, an equal and offsetting debit is recorded as a single line in the equity section. This reduces the net equity. This is referred to as the "ESOP Loan Contra Account" or "Unearned Compensation." Under ASC 718-40/ SOP 93-6, this contra account is called "Unearned ESOP Shares."

This contra-equity account is eliminated as the shares are allocated. The amount of reduction in the contra account for any year is measured by the amount of compensation expense recorded on the plan financial statements attributable to ESOP activity. The important point to recognize is that the unearned shares account will not necessarily be reduced at the same time or in the same amount that the ESOP loan balance is reduced. Where an ESOP loan uses the principal-only method of collateral release, the number of shares released is always directly tied to the principal reduction. But for GAAP, the shares are released when the employer commits to make the payment. The actual principal payment may be several months after the financial statement date. For a loan that applies the principal and interest method of collateral release, you will see this same timing difference on when shares are considered earned. There is an additional difference because the shares are released based upon both principal and interest payments. This means that shares are released and allocated at a different rate than principal is retired.

The ESOP's impact on retained earnings is reflected in three entries: compensation cost, tax effect, and dividends/S corporation distributions. These are described in more detail in the discussion below regarding the income statement effect of a leveraged ESOP. However, a portion of this activity does not flow through the income statement. That arises where dividends/S corporation distributions are paid on shares allocated to the accounts of the plan participant. These retain their character as true dividends.

The tax benefit from C corporation ESOP dividends paid on allocated shares is covered by ASC740-20-45-11(e)/SFAS 109. All of the tax benefit runs through the tax provision.

During 1989, another change was made in the manner that certain ESOPs may affect the equity section. This is described in ASC 480-10/ EITF Issue 89-11, "Sponsor's Balance Sheet Classification of Capital Stock with a Put Option Held by an Employee Stock Ownership Plan." This issue is generally considered to apply only to publicly traded enterprises, as it is based on the interpretation of SEC Accounting Release No. 268, "Presentation in Financial Statements of Redeemable Preferred Stocks." This release effectively provides that any stock held by an ESOP that is subject to a put option is to be classified outside of permanent capital. That is, it will be recorded into the portion on the right side of the balance sheet between debt and equity. This is frequently referred to as the "mezzanine" level. According to the EITF, the proportionate share of the contra-equity account attributable to these shares will also be recorded at this mezzanine level. These shares can remain in permanent equity if the plan sponsor can issue stock for the puts and has expressed the intent to do so. Any plan sponsor who makes this representation must realize that in that case, the SEC is likely to hold that the ESOP shares are common stock equivalents for purposes of calculating primary earnings per share. A key issue to understand about this mezzanine capital is that the stock is marked to market value. This is an area that may change as the FASB's work on financial instruments progresses. Currently, the one standard that addresses this issue, ASC 480-10/FAS 150, does not apply to stock held in an ESOP. See ASC 480-10-15-8/FASB Staff Position 150-4.

Before leaving the discussion of the ESOP's effect on the equity section, it is critical to note how inside loans, sometimes referred to as mirror loans, two-step loans, or back-to-back loans, affect the equity section. A simple inside loan is one in which the plan sponsor makes the loan to the plan without obtaining any related financing from the outside. The other terms describe situations in which the plan sponsor receives financing from the outside, then in turn loans funds to the ESOP. As noted earlier, however, the note receivable represented by the inside note between the plan sponsor and the ESOP is not recorded as an asset. Instead, that note receivable is what is reflected in the contra-equity account or Unearned ESOP Shares Account in the equity section of the balance sheet. As described above, it is not adjusted as collections are made on the note. Rather, it is adjusted as the associated shares are released for the benefit of employees.

Income Statement and Earnings per Share

The second financial statement in the typical set of financial statements is the income statement. When the original SOP was issued, there was as much controversy over the measurement of compensation expense in the income statement as there was over the recording of the debt. Basically, both controversies revolved around the same issue: Is the ESOP a compensation device, a financing device, or both? The accounting community is still wrestling with this issue. However, in publishing SOP 76-3, the AcSEC made the decision that it is both. That position has continued through the subsequent changes in ESOP accounting. Therefore, the income statement impact of an ESOP reflects a compensation cost and, if a direct loan is involved, an interest cost. (For purposes of this chapter, compensation expense and interest expense are discussed as though they are currently deductible. Any issues pertaining to whether some or all of one or the other need to be capitalized are outside of the scope of this discussion.)

There is no magic to the measurement of the interest expense. It is measured in the same manner as it would be for any other similar financial instrument.

The measurement of the compensation element is another story. Compensation cost is measured as shares are made available for allocation to plan participants. The dollar value of that compensation is based upon the current value of the shares to be allocated.

In 1977, the IRS and DOL released final regulations that provided that the ESOP participants would receive an annual allocation as the shares were released from collateral. These regulations established two methods of collateral release: the principal-and-interest method and the principal-only method. In the first case, shares are released from collateral and allocated to participants on the basis of the ratio of the current year's payment of principal and interest to the total of the current year's payments plus all future years' payments of principal and interest. The principal-only method is simply the ratio of the current year's principal payment to the total original principal of the loan. The principal-only method is limited by three specific requirements of the regulations. The major limit is to ESOP loans that at all times have cumulative principal payments of no less than a normal 10-year amortization loan.

The IRS regulations governing debt service refer to debt payments made "for" the plan year. This raises questions associated with when the release of shares is recognized for expense measurement. The standard calls for compensation cost to be measured by the number of shares "allocated, released or committed to be released" with respect to the reporting period. This means shares for which the debt has been paid, the shares have been released from collateral, and under the plan's terms they have been allocated to accounts of plan participants. It also covers shares where the loan payment has been made and the shares have been released, but, perhaps due to a difference in the plan year-end and the sponsor year-end, the shares have not yet been allocated. Finally, consistent with accrual accounting, it includes shares that will be released from collateral where the sponsor has committed to make a contribution with respect to the current year, but such contribution is to be paid in the subsequent year. The number of shares released for this purpose is controlled by the terms of the IRS regulations, the ESOP agreement, and the ESOP loan agreements.

The other key component to the measurement of compensation cost is the value assigned to these shares that have been allocated, released, or committed to be released. Under ASC 718-40-30-2/SOP 93-6 paragraph 16, compensation cost will be based on the average fair market value of the shares released or committed to be released with respect to any payments made on the ESOP debt for that year. This amount would be reduced by the dollar value of any dividends paid on allocated shares that have been applied to debt service. The average value for the year is used because the stock is assumed to have been earned throughout the year. As of the spring of 2012, the fair value concept for ESOPs was not based upon the evolving standard of fair value as defined in ASC 820/FAS 157. However, on October 14, 2011, the FASB announced a technical corrections project that proposed to replace the ESOP standard's definition of fair value with that used throughout the rest of GAAP. In most situations the ESOP concept of fair value under GAAP, whether ASC 820 or ASC 718-40 would match the ERISA standard. However in limited circumstances there may be a difference that would be significant for certain footnote disclosures. For example, consider an ESOP sponsored by a company whose stock is actively traded on the Over-the-Counter Bulletin Board. As defined in IRS Notice 2011-19, the IRS does not consider such shares to be traded in an established securities market and requires that the share value be based upon an appraisal. In those circumstances, GAAP (whether the new or old fair value standards) would likely conclude that the trading price is fair value. The ESOP trustee would consider the appraised price to be fair value. Where the financial statement reports the expense, the GAAP standard would apply and the footnotes could explain any difference. However, where the footnotes describe rights of the participants, such as the put option, their rights would be based upon the trustee's determination of value. In such circumstances, it would be critical to ensure that the correct fair value concept is used in the applicable accounting standard. Comments were filed with the FASB to make it aware of this issue as it considers the technical corrections project. The final conclusion of this project was not published at the time of this writing.

To illustrate how these rules apply to the measurement of ESOP compensation, consider the following example: An employer sponsors a 401(k) plan with a match. The match for the current plan year is $100,000. That match could be satisfied with the fair market value of employer securities released by the current year's contribution to the plan. Assume that the principal portion of the contribution required to release $100,000 of securities is only $80,000 (e.g., the company is using the principal-only method of collateral release, and the shares have increased in value by 25%). This is a direct ESOP loan, so both the financing and the compensation aspects of the entry must be recognized. The interest expense for the period on the ESOP note was $14,000.

The journal entries would be as follows to record the accrual of the matching contribution and interest:

Compensation cost	$100,000	
Interest expense	$14,000	
Accrued matching contribution		$100,000
Accrued interest payable		$14,000

In this fact pattern, the accrued contribution is recorded because the employer could decide to satisfy it with a cash contribution, rather than shares from the ESOP.

To record the payment of the match and the ESOP principal and interest and contra account, the increase in the market value of the stock is added to paid-in-capital:

Accrued matching contribution	$100,000	
Accrued interest payable	$14,000	
ESOP debt	$80,000	
Cash		$94,000
Unearned ESOP shares account		$80,000
Paid-in-capital		$20,000

If it were known that the matching contribution was to be satisfied through a contribution to the ESOP and associated release of shares, the accrued matching contribution would not be recorded. Instead, the following entries would have been made:

Compensation cost	$100,000	
Interest expense	$ 14,000	
Unearned ESOP shares account		$80,000
Paid-in-capital		$20,000
Accrued interest payable		$14,000

To record the accrued contribution/shares committed to be released and interest, the following entries would be made to record the payment to the ESOP of the cash and the ESOP's application of this cash to debt service:

ESOP debt	$80,000	
Accrued interest payable	$14,000	
Cash		$94,000

Dividends

Before leaving the discussion of the income statement, it is important to address the very unique treatment of dividends paid on employer securities held by a leveraged ESOP. (For the purposes of this discussion, distributions by an S corporation are included in the general concept of "dividend.")

Two provisions of the Internal Revenue Code (the "Code") have had significant influence on the design of ESOPs and thus a direct impact on the financial reporting for such plans. First, as long as the specific requirements of the Code and associated regulations are satisfied, dividends paid on leveraged shares may be applied to debt service. Second, dividends applied to debt service, distributed to plan participants, or subject to a cash-or-deferred election within the plan are tax deductible by a C corporation plan sponsor. For purposes of the dividend deduction, this is limited to dividends paid during the year. Dividends accrued at year-end are not eligible for this deduction until the later period in which they are paid.

In understanding the accounting rules for ESOP dividends, it is important to remember that the plan sponsor retains significant control over the application of dividends through its control over the drafting of plan terms and the negotiation of the ESOP loan agreements.

The financial reporting implications of dividends paid on ESOP shares varies between shares that are allocated or released to plan participants and those shares that remain as collateral, including shares that are committed to be released, on the loan to be released and allocated in future financial periods. This is a technical nuance that primarily applies to those shares that are released but unallocated and those committed to be released for the current period. To simplify the remainder of this discussion, the distinction will be allocated versus unallocated shares. Shares that are released but unallocated are treated as allocated. Shares committed to be released are classified as unallocated shares. See SOP 93-6 paragraph 77 because this comes from the basis-for-conclusions portion of the SOP; there is no equivalent paragraph in the ASC.

Dividends paid on allocated shares retain their character as true dividends. Where such dividends are applied to debt service, the compensation cost derived from the release of shares is reduced by the dollar amount of the dividends on allocated shares used to pay the debt. See ASC 718-40-25-16/SOP 93-6 paragraph 21. Where such dividends are tax-deductible, the tax benefit goes to reduce the current year's provision for taxes. See ASC 740-20-45-11(e).

Dividends paid on unallocated shares are always part of compensation cost. Where the cash attributable to such dividends is applied to debt service, these dividends become part of compensation through their impact on the number of shares released. Where such dividends are distributed to plan participants, part of the cash-or-deferred election, or simply retained in the trust to increase participant account balances, they are included in compensation cost. To the extent such dividends create compensation cost, the associated tax benefit, if any, is part of the current year's provision for taxes.

Earnings per Share

For nonleveraged ESOPs, all shares are considered outstanding, whether common or convertible preferred. For leveraged ESOPs, only the shares allocated, released, or committed to be released are considered outstanding. In all cases, convertible preferred stock is to be considered a common stock equivalent. This will reduce the number of shares considered outstanding until an ESOP loan is fully amortized. It is important to recognize that this result is for the GAAP reporting of earnings per share only. The shares still held as collateral remain outstanding for all other purposes—voting, determination of share value, etc.

Statements of Changes in Stockholders' Equity

The third financial statement consists of the Statements of Changes in Stockholders' Equity. Where the company sponsors a leveraged ESOP, a new column is added to this presentation to reflect the balance and changes in the balance of the Unearned ESOP Shares account. This statement would include columns for common or preferred stock, par value, additional paid-in-capital, unearned ESOP shares, and retained earnings. Only the columns applicable to the plan sponsor would be included. When ESOP shares are released from collateral and allocated to plan participants, each column is adjusted for the applicable effect. The Unearned ESOP Shares account is reduced by the release and allocation or is increased for additional leveraged purchases. The Retained Earnings account is adjusted for net income, which includes the impact of the ESOP compensation cost and for any dividends attributable to allocated shares. Market value changes on shares allocated, released, or committed to be released may adjust additional paid-in-capital, retained earnings, or stock depending upon the specific facts and circumstances of the plan sponsor.

Statements of Cash Flows

The fourth financial statement consists of the statements of cash flows. The existence of an ESOP does not change the content or the presentation of this financial statement. However, if the amount is material, there may be one or more line items included on this statement relative to the ESOP. If shares are contributed to the plan, they will be reflected as a non-cash expenditure. If the compensation cost reported varies materially from the cash contribution made to the plan, there will be a line item that reconciles from net income to cash flow from operations associated with that difference. Where a direct obligation of the ESOP is reflected on the financial statements of the plan sponsor, the payment of the debt is not reflected in the cash flow from financing activities because it is already reflected as a reduction in cash flow from operations. Where the ESOP is financed with an indirect loan from the plan sponsor, cash flow is not affected by the ESOP debt service, except for any tax benefit. This is because the plan sponsor contributes the cash to the ESOP to fund the debt, and the ESOP returns the same cash to the plan sponsor in repayment of its debt. Thus, the statement of cash flows from operations may reflect an add-back of the entire ESOP compensation cost.

The critical issue relating to the impact of a leveraged ESOP on the statements of cash flows goes more to the calculation of any loan covenants rather than the financial statement effect. Frequently, loan agreements include a concept of coverage. This relates to the ability of company cash flow to cover required payments on the debt. Where the debt is provided directly through the ESOP, cash flow from operations is reduced by the contribution to the ESOP. Thus, in defining the coverage ratio in the loan agreements, it is important to specifically account for this effect.

Footnote Disclosures

A general consensus of accounting authority recommends disclosure of the following information:

- A plan description, including the purpose, qualified status, contribution formula, method of releasing shares from collateral, and a description of the employer's securities held by the plan.

- A comparative table illustrating the number of allocated, released, committed to be released, and unallocated shares should be disclosed.

- The fair value of the unearned ESOP shares and the allocated shares as of the balance-sheet date.

- An ESOP loan description, including the terms, interest rate, and payment commitments.

- The amount of compensation recognized for the period.

- The method of measuring compensation expense, including dividends, if applicable.

- A disclosure of the repurchase commitment, e.g., the put option terms, for shares that are not publicly traded. To the extent that shares have been put to the employer before the end of the fiscal year but not yet paid, the liability would have to be booked, not just footnoted.

There is no current requirement to record or disclose the projected repurchase obligation, even if the amount is significant. Nor is any actuarial projection to be required for footnote disclosure. The only information required that relates to this concept is the requirement to disclose the fair value of all allocated shares.

Special Issues

Book/Tax Differences

Where the plan sponsor is faced with material amounts of income tax liabilities, GAAP requires recognition of the deferred tax effects that arise when income or expense is recognized at a different time for financial statements than for income tax reporting. This is a very complex standard governed by ASC 740. When accumulating the information to present the current and deferred tax effects on the plan sponsor's financial statements, the following effects of the leveraged ESOP are to be considered:

1. Compensation cost is measured by the average fair market value of the shares released for GAAP. The deduction for tax purposes is the cash contributed to the plan to service the debt. This results in one or two book tax differences: (a) the difference between the original cost of the shares and the market value is a permanent difference, or (b) the difference between the original cost of the shares and the principal payment is a timing difference.

2. For GAAP reporting, the interest is excluded on indirect loans, but for tax purposes, the interest expense of the ESOP loan is part of the contribution deduction. The interest paid to the employer in repayment of the loan is interest income to the employer. This is just a classification difference. There may, however, be a timing difference as the interest reported for GAAP is that attributable to

the financial statement period. For tax purposes, the contribution may include interest through the due date of the tax return, including extensions.

Contributions Paid in Advance of Required Debt Service

This is an issue that is not included in GAAP, but consensus has been reached among most accountants. It is not uncommon for a company to set up an ESOP in year 1 and make a contribution for that year, but not close the leveraged transaction until the following year. Alternatively, a cash contribution in excess of what is required for current debt service might be made to provide extra liquidity in the ESOP in the event that the sponsor experiences a cash shortage in a later year. These amounts are part of compensation cost for the year paid or accrued. They are required to be allocated to participant accounts for that period. However, where the appropriate documentation has been provided to the plan fiduciary, it is possible for such cash amounts to be applied to debt service in a later year. In such event, the normal rule that compensation expense is measured by the average fair value of the shares released for that period would result in the double-counting of compensation. It would have been recorded in the year of the contribution and again in the year that the funds were applied to debt service. To avoid this issue, there is a simple result. The compensation expense for the year that this cash is applied to debt service is reduced by the amount that has previously been included in expense.

ESOPs in Leveraged Buyouts

Accounting for ESOP transactions becomes particularly complicated when the ESOP is a party to a leveraged buyout of an entity. In these situations, the ESOP accounting complexities are added to the purchase accounting issues presented by any business combination. This discussion is outside the scope of this chapter. It is critical to recognize that the business combination rules basically are applied first to the reporting, and the impact of the ESOP as a provider of some of the financing is only then integrated into the reporting. Where preferred shares are used or where shares are transferred over a period of time, special rules may apply.

S Corporations

Since the law was changed in 1998 to permit S corporations to have an ESOP as a shareholder, many ESOP sponsors have elected S corporation status. An S corporation does not pay federal or most state income taxes directly. Rather, taxable income is passed through to shareholders, who then pay tax or not based upon their own tax situation. Under current law, an ESOP is exempt from tax on income passed through from an S corporation as long as a variety of technical requirements are satisfied.

The S election does not change the format of the financial statements, nor does it change the general rules described above for the accounting of ESOP transactions. However, there are some unique financial reporting consequences to an S election that need to be considered:

1. When a company changes to S corporation status, deferred taxes do not have to be recognized for any temporary book/tax differences occurring after the date of the change in tax status, except in the case of post-1986 S corporation elections discussed below. When a company converts from C corporation status to S corporation status, it must retain any material existing deferred tax liability to the extent it would be subject to built-in gains tax. The deferred tax liability will continue to be remeasured at each balance sheet date until the end of the 10-year period. Any other deferred tax amounts are eliminated as of the date of change from C to S status.

2. Under the Revenue Act of 1987, a company with LIFO inventories electing S corporation status after December 17, 1987, will include its LIFO reserve in its last return filed as a C corporation. The tax is payable in equal amounts over four years, with the first payment due by the due date (not including extensions) of the last return filed as a C corporation. The total liability should be accrued and charged to income tax expense applicable to income from continuing operations at the date of change. When a company is subject to the LIFO recapture requirement, the LIFO recapture represents a new LIFO base for income tax purposes. However, for financial statement purposes the LIFO recapture requirement does not affect the LIFO base. Accordingly, it will be necessary for those affected companies to maintain LIFO

cost records separately for income tax and financial statement purposes.

3. Similar rules to the LIFO recapture apply to financial institutions with respect to bad debt reserves. The built-in gains rules are also more complicated for financial institutions.

4. There is no tax benefit associated with such dividends. Thus, the financial reporting consequences for debt payments from S corporation distributions are easier to understand and to apply.

5. Because other plan terms may also change with the election of S status, the footnote disclosures for the ESOP may change.

Esops and ASC 810/FIN 46R: Variable Interest Entities

One of the most frustrating things that face ESOP sponsors is when their advisors do not agree on some technical issue. Generally, such disagreements arise in situations where the guidance is subject to different interpretations. The topic of variable interest entities is apparently one of those areas. Under GAAP, where a company has a holding in a "variable interest entity," the financial results of that entity must be reflected on the financial statements of the holder. As is the case when an ESOP is a party to a leveraged buyout of an entity, this is a very technical subject beyond the scope of this chapter. However, because of the varying interpretations on the application of this standard, it is important to highlight the basis for these interpretations.

ASC 810 does not apply to a benefit plan that is accounted for under ASC 715/FAS 87. Those parties who hold that leveraged ESOPs are subject to assessment under the variable interest entity standard believe that SOP 93-6 is a separate standard, independent of FAS 87. Those parties who conclude that the variable interest entity rules do not apply to a leveraged ESOP believe that SOP 93-6 is merely an interpretation of FAS 87, as was required to consider the implications of unallocated assets within a benefit plan trust.

I was a party to the drafting of SOP 93-6. During the FASB hearings on what eventually became SOP 93-6, specific comments were made as to whether the expense recognition would be controlled by principles similar to option reporting under what was then APB

25 or the principles of FAS 87. It was concluded in those hearings that because the ESOP is a qualified defined contribution plan, the principles articulated in FAS 87 controlled. However, this conclusion did not come through very clearly in the final draft of the SOP, as the references to existing standards simply say that the SOP is consistent with FAS 87 with respect to the accounting for nonleveraged ESOPs. It is likely that when the components of the financial presentation are compared, there may not be a lot of difference between the financial results with or without variable interest entity treatment. However, to avoid controversy, the plan sponsor should resolve this matter with its advisors at implementation.

Practical Applications

As tables 3-1 and 3-2 illustrate, the impact of a leveraged ESOP on a company's balance sheet is dramatic. Financial ratios, like debt to equity, are substantially affected. This case was fairly minor, as it anticipated that the capital would stay in the company. When the capital is leaving the company to repurchase the stock of a retiring shareholder, circumstances become even more exotic. In this case, it is not at all unusual to see a negative equity section.

In many cases the "adverse" consequences of the accounting treatment can be minimized through a well-planned transaction. In some cases, the accounting rules cannot be managed. For example, until the users of statements become more sophisticated, the ESOP accounting rules simply will not allow for a highly leveraged ESOP that is used to retire a former owner in an enterprise whose ability to do business is a current function of its equity section, for example, an enterprise subject to bonding or a financial institution. In all cases, the accounting needs to be discussed at the beginning of the transaction, not after closing.

Alternative options are available for companies that could not tolerate the accounting consequences of recording the ESOP debt on the balance sheet and the offsetting, negative impact on the equity section. Unfortunately, these alternatives require the loss of some ESOP advantages in exchange for the less objectionable accounting treatment.

Table 3-1. Traditional Leveraged ESOP

Balance sheet pre-ESOP

		Accounts payable	$30,000
		Bank debt	10,000
		Total liabilities	$40,000
		Stockholders' equity	70,000
Total assets	$110,000	Total liability and stockholders' equity	$110,000

Balance sheet post-ESOP

		Accounts payable	$30,000
		Bank debt	10,000
		ESOP debt	1,000
		Total liabilities	$41,000
		Stockholders' equity	$71,000
		ESOP contra account	(1,000)
		Total stockholders' equity	$70,000
Total assets	$111,000	Total liability and stockholders' equity	$111,000

Balance sheet post-ESOP, year 2

No changes except the payment of principal on ESOP note. Assume no profit or loss before contribution of principal (compensation expense) and interest. The principal-only method of collateral release is used. Therefore, compensation expense equals principal payment.

		Accounts payable	$30,000
		Bank debt	10,000
		ESOP debt	900
		Total liabilities	$40,900
		Stockholders' equity	$71,000
		ESOP contra account	(900)
		Current year's loss	(200)
		Total stockholders' equity	$69,900
Total assets	$110,800	Total liability and stockholders' equity	$110,800

Table 3-2. Two-Step ESOP Loan		
Balance sheet pre-ESOP		
	Accounts payable	$30,000
	Bank debt	10,000
	Total liabilities	$40,000
	Stockholders' equity	70,000
Total assets $110,000	Total liability and stockholders' equity	$110,000
Balance sheet post-ESOP		
	Accounts payable	$30,000
	Bank debt	11,000
	Total liabilities	$41,000
	Stockholders' equity	$71,000
	ESOP receivable	(1,000)
	Total stockholders' equity	$70,000
Total assets $110,000	Total liability and stockholders' equity	$111,000

Nonleveraged ESOP

Under this approach, the ESOP does not use debt financing to purchase the shares. Instead, an annual cash contribution is made to the plan, which it uses to purchase shares or the plan sponsor simply contributes shares to the plan. Since there is no ESOP debt in this case, there is no need to record the debt or the offsetting contra-equity entry. However, this transaction means that there is not a single purchase of stock that qualifies for all the leveraged ESOP incentives. Instead, there will be a series of purchases that may eventually qualify for certain ESOP incentives.

The primary cash flow advantage of an ESOP, namely deductible principal payments, can be simulated with this approach. Assume a company needed $1 million in additional capital. It could borrow the funds from a lender under a typical commercial loan. As annual principal payments are required, the company could contribute shares to the ESOP with a value equal to that year's principal payment. Assuming that the contribution was within the limitations of Section 404(a)(3) of the

Code, the company would get a tax deduction for a noncash expense, the contribution of stock. Thus its cash flow picture would be exactly the same as if the ESOP had borrowed the $1 million and the company had made a plan contribution sufficient to amortize the debt. (However, a leveraged ESOP may offer more tax incentives, as discussed in the first chapter of this book.)

Partially Leveraged ESOP

In some cases, plan sponsors have some flexibility in taking on ESOP financing, but they cannot take the entire piece in one year. In these transactions, a combination of the nonleveraged plan and a smaller leveraged plan can be used. For example, rather than a single purchase of 30% of the company, three separate sales of 10% each are arranged over a period of years. The seller cannot obtain the tax-deferred sale benefit on the first two sales, but the tradeoff is that the transaction can be handled without the major negative entry into the equity section and the disruption of the plan sponsor's bonding capacity or other business operations that are based on the equity section.

Conclusion

The advantages of ESOPs can be maximized and the disadvantages minimized with proper planning. A clear picture of what the accounting effects of an ESOP will be should be considered at the earliest possible stage of planning for an ESOP.

The financial reporting for ESOP transactions has been and continues to be in a state of change. As such, ESOP sponsors and corporations contemplating the implementation of an ESOP need to be sensitive to this.

Chapter 4

Section 1042 and the Tax-Deferred ESOP "Rollover"

Scott Rodrick[1]

One of the main uses of an ESOP is to buy out the shareholders of a closely held company. An ESOP is ideally suited to that task for various reasons: for example, it provides a ready market for the selling shareholders' shares; shareholders can sell in stages instead of all at once; it preserves continuity at the company by not bringing in a third-party buyer who may disrupt operations (e.g., by firing people or selling off parts of the company); employees are given a new retirement plan that, in conjunction with a participative management approach, can produce notable performance gains; and the company receives tax deductions for its contributions to the ESOP.

But there is yet another factor that drives many ESOP transactions: the tax-deferred "ESOP rollover." Under Internal Revenue Code ("Code") Section 1042, the shareholders of a closely held C corporation can indefinitely postpone taxation on the gain resulting from the ESOP sale to the extent they reinvest ("roll over") the sale proceeds in securities of U.S. operating corporations. Nobody likes to pay taxes, even at the lower long-term capital gains rates, and the savings afforded by the "ESOP rollover" are a powerful incentive for prospective sellers to an ESOP.[2] Most states recognize Section 1042, so the tax-deferred rollover

---

1. The author thanks James Steiker of Steiker, Fischer, Edwards & Greenapple, P.C.; Michael Coffey of Corporate Capital Resources LLC; and Keith Apton of UBS for their assistance in revising this chapter.

2. The tax-deferred "ESOP rollover" for the seller under Section 1042 should not be confused with the rollover of an ESOP distribution into an ESOP participant's IRA or other qualified benefit plan.

it provides is particularly valuable in high-tax states where the seller can avoid both federal and state taxes under this provision.[3]

The Section 1042 Rules in Brief

Section 1042 was not originally part of ESOP law. It was added to the Code by the Tax Reform Act of 1984.[4] It does not apply automatically; rather, the selling shareholder must affirmatively elect Section 1042 treatment. *§ 1042 requires an affirmative election*

This chapter will begin with a brief summary of the rules for the tax deferral and then follow with a more detailed discussion of each point. Most of these rules are contained in Section 1042 and other sections of the Code, but others are in temporary regulations promulgated by the Internal Revenue Service (IRS) in 1986. Also note that not all of these rules apply to the seller. Namely, violating the requirements for the ESOP to avoid allocating stock from the 1042 transaction to certain individuals and to avoid disposing of the stock within three years results in excise taxes to the company, but such prohibited allocations and prohibited dispositions of the stock do not disqualify the tax deferral for the shareholder(s) who sold to the ESOP in the transaction.

- The company sponsoring the ESOP must be a closely held C corporation, not a publicly traded company or an S corporation.

- The ESOP must own at least 30% of the common equity of the company after the transaction.

- The selling shareholder cannot be a C corporation but rather must be an individual, trust, estate, partnership, or limited liability company (LLC), or perhaps an S corporation.

---

3. For example, California Revenue and Taxation Code Section 18042 specifies in part that "Section 1042 of the Internal Revenue Code, relating to sales of stock to employee stock ownership plans or certain cooperatives, shall apply to taxable years beginning on or after January 1, 1995."

4. Section 1042 applies not only to ESOPs but also to certain worker-owned cooperatives. This discussion will focus on ESOPs because this book is about ESOPs. Additionally, Section 1042 is almost always used for ESOPs.

- The stock sold to the ESOP must have been held by the seller for at least three years before the sale. (When stock ownership is exchanged for a prior partnership or LLC interest, the total time of ownership is measured, as described below.)

- The stock sold to the ESOP must *not* have been acquired through a qualified retirement plan (such as an ESOP) or through a stock option or discounted employee stock purchase arrangement.

- The stock sold to the ESOP must be common stock with certain voting power and dividend rights, or preferred stock convertible into such common stock.

- During a period starting three months before the sale and ending a year after the sale, the seller must reinvest ("roll over") the proceeds or an equivalent sum of money (in any amount up to the amount of the sale) in "qualified replacement property" (QRP) (basically, the securities of U.S. operating companies).

- With certain exceptions, if the ESOP disposes of any of the stock within three years after the sale, the company must pay a 10% excise tax.

- For at least ten years after the sale, the ESOP must not allocate stock bought in the sale to the ESOP accounts of the seller or certain relatives of the seller. With no time limitation, the ESOP must not allocate such stock to any more-than-25% shareholders or to related parties of more-than-25% shareholders deemed to hold stock by attribution. Otherwise, the company must pay a 50% excise tax, and the person receiving the allocation is currently taxable on the value of the allocation.

- After the sale, the seller must file the following two documents with the seller's income tax return for the year in which the sale occurs:

  1. A "statement of election" under which the seller elects tax-deferred treatment.

  2. A verified statement from the company consenting to the imposition of the 10% and 50% excise taxes referred to above if the ESOP disposes of the stock within three years after the sale or makes a prohibited allocation.

Furthermore, every time the seller purchases QRP, the seller must obtain:

3. A notarized "statement of purchase," which then must be filed as discussed below. (If the QRP has been bought at the time of the Section 1042 election, the statement(s) of purchase must be filed along with the statement of election.)

The Section 1042 Rules in Detail

Nature of the ESOP Sponsor

Section 1042 applies only to sales to an ESOP established in a domestic C corporation.[5] For at least one year before and immediately after the sale, the company, and each corporation that is a member of the same controlled group of corporations with the company as defined in Code Section 409(l), must have no stock outstanding that is readily tradable on an established securities market.[6]

Shareholders selling to an ESOP in an S corporation cannot take advantage of Section 1042. An S corporation that wishes to make the Section 1042 "rollover" available to its shareholders may terminate its S corporation election, thus converting to C status.[7] A company wishing to elect S status may stay a C corporation long enough for the tax-deferred sale to the ESOP to take place, and then elect S status the year after the sale.

The 30% Requirement

Immediately after the sale, the ESOP must own at least 30% of either each class of outstanding stock or the total value of all outstanding stock (excluding in both cases nonconvertible, nonvoting preferred stock, but including stock constructively owned through options, warrants,

---

5. Code § 1042(c)(1)(A).

6. Ibid.; Code § 409(l); Temp. Treas. Reg. § 1.1042-1T, Q&A-1(b).

7. No delay is needed after termination of the S election. In PLR 200003014 (Oct. 20, 1999), the IRS ruled that a seller could undertake a Section 1042 sale immediately after the company changed from a S corporation to a C corporation.

or convertible debentures).[8] Section 1042 transactions are often accomplished through a sale of convertible preferred stock representing more than 30% of the *value* of all company stock but less than 30% of the outstanding common stock upon conversion. Note that the ESOP need not own any stock before the sale.

Sales to the ESOP by two or more shareholders can be treated as a single sale meeting the 30% requirement if they are "part of a single, integrated transaction under a prearranged agreement" between the sellers.[9]

Who Can Sell to the ESOP and Elect 1042 Treatment

Usually, the selling shareholders who elect Section 1042 are individuals. They also can be partnerships, trusts,[10] estates, or limited liability companies (LLCs). They cannot, however, be C corporations, and it is unclear whether they can be S corporations.[11] If the seller is a partnership or LLC, it is the partnership or LLC itself, not individual partners or members, that makes the Section 1042 election and purchases the QRP.[12]

---

8.   Code § 1042(b)(2). Section 1042(b)(2) applies the attribution rules of Code Section 318(a)(4), under which someone with an option to acquire stock is treated as owning such stock. The term "option" in Section 318(a)(4) includes warrants and convertible debentures when they are redeemable at the election of the holder. Rev. Ruls. 68-601, 1968-2 C.B. 124, and 89-64, 1989-1 C.B. 91.

9.   Temp. Treas. Reg. § 1.1042-1T, Q&A-2(b).

10. Section 1042(a)(1) specifies that the "taxpayer" elects 1042 treatment. A trust can sell to an ESOP and elect Section 1042 where it is the taxpayer (e.g., not a revocable grantor trust), as in PLR 9143013 (July 18, 1991). In PLR 200337003 (Sept. 12, 2003), where stock had been transferred to revocable grantor trusts and was to be sold to an ESOP, the "taxpayers" who could elect Section 1042 treatment and purchase QRP were the grantors, not the trusts.

11. Code § 1042(c)(7) (regarding C corporations). Section 1042 does not specifically exclude S corporations from acting as selling shareholders in this context. However, in 2001, during discussions leading to an ESOP-related private letter ruling, the IRS firmly rejected a suggestion by the ESOP practitioners requesting the PLR that an S corporation could sell to an ESOP and elect tax-deferred 1042 treatment. The practitioners then withdrew that issue from their PLR request. Also, it is unusual for an S corporation to own C corporation stock in the first place.

12. Technical Advice Memorandum 9508001 (Oct. 13, 1994) and PLR 9846005 (Nov. 13, 1998) (dealing with partnerships); PLR 200243001 (Oct. 25, 2002)

tacking rules

Nature of the Stock Sold in a 1042 Transaction

The stock sold to the ESOP must have been held by the seller for at least three years before the ESOP transaction, determined as of the time of the sale.[13]

To reach the three-year holding requirement, a seller who has held the stock for less than three years may take advantage of the "tacking" rules in Section 1223 of the Code. These rules allow the seller, in certain circumstances, to "tack" on the holding period of an asset that was exchanged for the stock in a transaction where both the stock and the asset for which it was exchanged have the same basis (i.e., a gift or tax-free exchange).[14]

The gain on the sale of stock sold to the ESOP must be otherwise eligible for long-term capital gain treatment, i.e., it cannot be stock that is ineligible for capital gain treatment, such as preferred stock subject to Code Section 306.

The stock sold to the ESOP must not have been acquired through a qualified retirement plan (such as an ESOP), through exercising stock options, or through restricted stock or discounted stock purchase arrangements under Section 83 of the Code.[15]

The stock sold to the ESOP must be (1) common stock having a combination of voting power and dividend rights equal to or in excess of (a) the class of common stock having the greatest voting power and (b) the class of common stock having the greatest dividend rights, or (2) preferred stock convertible into such common stock at a reasonable conversion price.[16] (Note: this is not a Section 1042 requirement but

---

(dealing with an LLC). Note: for federal tax purposes, an LLC is generally treated as a partnership.

13. Code § 1042(b)(4).

14. Douglas Jaques, "'Tacking' On to the Section 1042 Seller's Holding Period," *Journal of Employee Ownership Law and Finance* 8, no. 1 (winter 1996): 29.

15. Code § 1042(c)(1)(B). Although the statute is unclear on this point, many ESOP practitioners think that stock acquired at fair market value (or above) in an employee stock purchase arrangement should be eligible for Section 1042 sales. However, at least one IRS representative has informally stated that this is not the case and that absolutely no stock acquired through an employee stock purchase arrangement may be sold to an ESOP in a Section 1042 transaction.

16. Code §§ 1042(c)(1), 409(l).

rather is a general requirement for most ESOP tax incentives applicable to closely held companies.)

Qualified Replacement Property (QRP)

To obtain the Section 1042 tax deferral, the seller must reinvest proceeds of the sale in QRP during a period beginning 3 months before and ending 12 months after the date of the sale, i.e., the date the stock is sold to the ESOP.[17] The tax deferral lasts as long as the seller holds the QRP (this is discussed more below).

QRP Need Not Be Bought with the Actual ESOP Sale Proceeds

The IRS does not trace the funds from the sale; as is apparent from the "3 months before" aspect of this rule, the actual funds from the sale need not be used. For example, a seller who has $1 million to invest can buy QRP three months before the ESOP transaction, receive $1 million in the transaction, and freely invest or spend the $1 million in proceeds from the actual sale.

The Seller Can Elect Section 1042 Treatment for Any Amount of the Proceeds

Also note that the seller can elect Section 1042 treatment for any amount of the sale proceeds. Of course, this means that the seller will pay capital gains taxes on the amount not reinvested under Section 1042. Thus, a selling shareholder might receive $1 million from an ESOP transaction, reinvest half of it in QRP and elect Section 1042 treatment for that amount, and spend the other half (or rather what remains of it after paying capital gains taxes) on a new house.

What QRP Can and Cannot Be

The QRP itself must consist of securities issued by a domestic operating corporation. "Securities" in this context includes stock; rights to subscribe for or to receive stock; and bonds, debentures, notes, certificates, or other evidence of indebtedness issued by a corporation, with interest coupons

---

17. Code § 1042(c)(3).

NO REITS, mutual funds or P/ships

No Gov't Securities

or in registered form.[18] A domestic corporation is one incorporated in the U.S.[19] Section 1042 defines an "operating corporation" as one where more than 50% of the company's assets were used in the active conduct of a business as of the time the security was purchased or before the end of the 15-month period for buying QRP. No more than 25% of the corporation's gross income can come from passive investment income.[20] However, shares in financial institutions defined as banks in Code Section 581 and in insurance companies subject to taxation are specifically designated as "operating companies" under Section 1042 and thus are excluded from the passive income rule.[21] Government securities cannot be QRP.[22]

The rollover securities need to qualify as QRP only when the seller buys them and elects to treat them as QRP. If, for example, a seller buys a company's stock as QRP and a few years later the company becomes a non-operating company or reincorporates in a foreign country, the seller can keep holding the stock as QRP.

The QRP must consist of the actual securities themselves, not mutual funds. Real estate investment trusts (REITs) and partnership interests also are off-limits.

There is no prohibition against reinvesting in securities of closely held companies, but the QRP cannot include securities of the ESOP company itself—that is, the company whose shares were sold to the ESOP (e.g., a shareholder in Company X cannot sell 30% of Company X's stock to Company X's new ESOP and then buy more Company X stock to serve as QRP). Corporations controlled by the ESOP company or that own stock representing control of the ESOP company are also excluded from being QRP.[23] However, it would be permissible for the QRP to consist of shares in another company owned by the seller that was not in the same controlled group of corporations, including a new corporation funded wholly with the ESOP sale proceeds.[24]

---

18. Code Sections 1042(c)(4)(D) and 165(g)(2).
19. This would include a U.S. subsidiary of a foreign corporation.
20. Code § 1042(c)(4)(A)-(B).
21. Code § 1042(c)(4)(B)(ii).
22. Code § 1042(c)(4)(D).
23. Code § 1042(c)(4)(C).
24. PLR 9720026 (Feb. 12, 1997).

Investing in Floating-Rate Notes (ESOP Notes) as QRP

One strategy that investment advisors have devised for clients who have elected 1042 treatment is to use floating-rate notes (sometimes called "ESOP Notes") that have been offered for this purpose. These are long-term highly rated corporate bonds, often with a maturity of 30 to 50 years, that pay an adjustable rate of interest pegged to short-term LIBOR rates. (When a bond matures, is called, or is sold, that constitutes a disposition of the QRP, which in turn triggers the capital gains taxes that the QRP investment was intended to delay in the first place.) The appeal of this investment is that the floating-rate notes theoretically have low credit risk and low interest rate risk and therefore can be used as collateral for borrowing at a very high ratio to their value. These notes usually come with both a put and call feature. The call feature is designed to eliminate the risk of the note being called away, which would create a disposition of the QRP, and the put feature allows the QRP investor to sell the note back to the issuer as needed at a specified price and date outlined in the prospectus.

The selling shareholder can often borrow 80% to 90% of the value of the floating-rate note and invest the borrowed sums freely while still deferring taxes on the original sale to the ESOP, which has considerable appeal for some individuals. However, there are costs involved to set up the transaction, and to benefit from this strategy, the investor must (after any brokerage and management fees) generate higher returns with the amount that was borrowed than he or she would with 100% of the sale proceeds invested in a conventional buy-and-hold QRP portfolio. Additionally, in a credit crisis a floating-rate note may lose much of its value (as happened in 2008 for QRP investors who had bought AIG notes), which could trigger a margin call, although after such a crisis the notes may regain their value. In the event of a margin call, the QRP investor might be forced to liquidate part of the QRP if he or she is unable to deposit the cash necessary to cure the margin call. This cash will be released back to the investor if the bond regains its value after the markets settle or its credit regains its footing. Should the investor be forced to liquidate part of the floating-rate note holdings, this would create a taxable event not for the full deferral, but for the portion of the QRP that was sold.

The possibility of a credit crisis makes the use of floating-rate notes questionable for seller-financed transactions where the shareholder lacks the assets to meet a margin call. Banks providing monetization loans secured by QRP have taken this into consideration since the 2008 financial crisis by requiring annual personal financial statements showing that the client has the means to meet a margin call should one occur. The risk of a margin call, however, can be minimized through creating a diverse portfolio of floating-rate notes instead of only using a single issuer.[25]

Accordingly, the floating-rate note QRP strategy may be best suited for younger, aggressive investors who have several million dollars or more to invest in QRP, who are ready to deal with the costs and risks this strategy entails, and who create a diverse portfolio of floating-rate notes from multiple issuers.[26] For such investors, the flexibility that the floating-rate note strategy provides can help mitigate risk in changing capital markets.

General QRP Investment Strategies

Selling shareholders should not feel compelled to follow a special investment strategy such as buying floating-rate notes and borrowing against them. In many cases, sellers and their advisors conclude the best strategy is simply to invest in stocks and bonds that qualify as QRP and that would be good long-term investments regardless of their status as QRP. At any rate, sellers are advised to use qualified investment advisors

---

25. As an illustration, after the collapse of Lehman Brothers in September 2008, the value of the AIG floating-rate note dropped to 70 cents per dollar. This created a margin call for many investors. For those that had a diversified portfolio this caused little harm, as the margin call was on a small percentage of the portfolio. For those that had a heavy concentration in financials, including AIG, this created a much greater problem, as the impact of the margin call was much larger. However, AIG did honor the put price of 98 cents on the dollar for many of the securities that individual floating-rate note investors held. The sale of the note back to AIG was a disposition of QRP and thus a taxable event, the impact of which was relatively small when the AIG floating-rate note was just a small part of a broad QRP portfolio.

26. For a detailed discussion of floating-rate notes as QRP, see Keith J. Apton and Michael A. Coffey, "The Section 1042 Rollover," in *Selling Your Business to an ESOP*, 9th ed. (Oakland, CA: NCEO, 2012), 127–29.

to avoid traps such as investing in a seemingly eligible U.S. company that fails to qualify as QRP because it had too much passive income.

Donating the QRP to a Charitable Remainder Trust

The selling shareholder may invest the sale proceeds in QRP (thereby avoiding capital gains taxes) and then donate some or all of that QRP to a charitable remainder trust (CRT). In return, the shareholder receives a tax deduction plus annual income for the remainder of the shareholder's life, for the lives of the shareholder and his or her spouse, or for a fixed period. The gift is irrevocable, however, and thus the shareholder's heirs will not inherit the QRP. Another option is for the shareholder to avoid selling to the ESOP and instead contribute the stock to a CRT, which then may sell to the ESOP.[27]

When (and Whether) Tax Is Due Upon Disposition of QRP

As noted above, when the seller disposes of any QRP, the gain that was deferred is now realized, and the seller must pay taxes on the portion of the deferred gain that the sale represents.[28] The basis of the QRP is the basis the seller's stock had when it was sold to the ESOP.[29] However, no gain is realized if the stock is exchanged for stock of another company

---

27. For details, see Apton and Coffey, "The Section 1042 Rollover," 129–31.

28. Code § 1042(e)(1).

29. Code § 1042(d). Literally, the taxpayer's basis in the QRP is reduced by the gain not recognized due to the 1042 election, so the basis of the stock sold to the ESOP becomes the basis of the QRP. This means that if the QRP loses value and is sold, the seller may still owe taxes. For example, say that the owner's basis in the stock is $200,000, and he sells it to the ESOP for its fair market value of $1 million. To avoid paying taxes on the $800,000 gain, he reinvests the $1 million in stocks of 10 companies at $100,000 each and elects Section 1042 treatment. Under Code Section 1042(d), the unrecognized gain of $800,000 reduces his $1 million basis in the QRP to the $200,000 level of the stock sold to the ESOP, allocated pro-rata to each of the investments. Years later, the value of one of the $100,000 QRP investments has fallen to $50,000, and the seller disposes of the stock. Although he lost half of his $100,000 investment in this portion of the QRP, its basis is $20,000 (i.e., its pro-rata portion of the $200,000 basis in the stock sold to the ESOP), and he now owes taxes on $30,000 (the difference between the $50,000 in proceeds from the sale of the QRP and the $20,000 basis of the QRP).

in a tax-free corporate reorganization under Code Section 368, by reason of the seller's death, by gift (such as a charitable contribution, or a transfer to a charitable remainder trust or to the seller's relatives[30]), or in another transaction to which Section 1042 applies.[31] And if a seller holds QRP when he or she dies, the heirs receive a basis in the QRP that is stepped-up to the fair market value of the stock at the time of death,[32] thus achieving a complete avoidance of taxation on the proceeds of the sale to the ESOP.

Some sellers have the misconception that holding QRP is like holding stock in a tax-deferred account such as an IRA, where dividends and interest on the assets held in the account are not taxable. This is not the case with QRP: the tax deferral applies only to the proceeds from the sale to the ESOP, and all earnings from the QRP are taxed.

Similarly, sellers should remember that tax is due only on the QRP that has been disposed of. Thus, a seller may elect Section 1042 and make small sales of QRP over time to rebalance his or her portfolio, paying the appropriate tax upon each disposition. Along the same lines, sellers should remember that even a short- or medium-term tax deferral may be useful in a given situation.

Using the QRP as Collateral

The section above on investing in floating-rate notes as QRP discusses using the notes as collateral for a loan to the *seller* so the seller can invest the borrowed money outside the constraints of Section 1042. In an entirely different context, some or all of the QRP can be pledged as collateral for a bank loan in the ESOP transaction itself. The chapter on ESOP underwriting considerations in this book discusses this in detail.

The ESOP's Three-Year Holding Period

If the ESOP disposes of any stock within three years after the sale, the company must pay a 10% excise tax on the amount realized by the ESOP

---

30. In PLR 201024005 (June 18, 2010), the IRS ruled that a selling shareholder's transfer of QRP to his spouse in connection with their divorce was not a disposition because it constituted a gift.

31. Code § 1042(e)(3).

32. Code § 1014.

on the disposition. The IRS does not trace the particular shares that were sold. Rather, the law imposes the tax if, after the disposition in question, either (1) the total number of shares in the ESOP is now less than the total number that the ESOP held immediately after the sale, or (2) the value of the stock held by the ESOP is now less than 30% of the value of all employer securities as of the date of the disposition.[33]

The foregoing rule does not apply to an exchange of stock by the ESOP for stock of another corporation in certain tax-free reorganizations, or to benefit distributions due to termination of employment or in connection with ESOP diversification requirements.[34]

The Prohibited Allocation Rule

If the selling shareholder elects the Section 1042 tax deferral, the ESOP is prohibited from making allocations of stock from that transaction to the seller, more-than-25% shareholders, and certain relatives. If the company wishes to compensate key employees who are prohibited from receiving ESOP allocations under the this rule, it cannot use a tax-qualified retirement plan meeting the requirements of Code Section 401(a) to allocate shares or other benefits in place of the prohibited ESOP shares.[35] Instead, the company must use plans such as stock options (including tax-qualified options), restricted stock, phantom stock, stock appreciation rights (SARs), and direct stock purchases.[36]

Prohibition on Allocations to Sellers and Related Individuals

For a "nonallocation period" of the later of (1) 10 years after the sale or (2) after the allocation of stock attributable to the final loan repayment if it was a leveraged transaction, the ESOP cannot make allocations of

---

33. Code § 4978(a)-(b).

34. Code § 4978(d). To be precise, Section 4978(d) refers not to termination in general but specifically to distributions due to death, disability, retirement after age 59½, and separation from service resulting in a one-year break in service.

35. Code § 409(n)(1).

36. The discussion here summarizes the rules in brief; for a more detailed discussion, see Brian B. Snarr, "The Prohibited Allocation Rule Under Section 1042," in *Selling Your Business to an ESOP*, 9th ed. (Oakland, CA: NCEO, 2012), to which the author is indebted.

stock from the 1042 transaction to the selling shareholder and anyone related to the seller as defined by Code Section 267(b).[37] Among family members, such related individuals include only siblings, spouses, ancestors, and lineal descendants (including legally adopted children),[38] and thus do not include aunts and uncles, etc.

Other Section 1042 Sellers

The IRS held in a private letter ruling that where several people sold to the company's ESOP and elected Section 1042 treatment, and one was an ESOP participant (who was unrelated to the other sellers), that participant was prohibited from receiving any allocations of any ESOP shares, not just the ones he sold to the ESOP. The IRS stated that "none of the shareholders who sold . . . stock to the ESOP may receive an allocation . . . because [they] all . . . elected the application of [S]ection 1042(a)." The applicable "nonallocation period" was the one for selling shareholders as stated in the paragraph above (the later of 10 years or after the final stock allocation when the loan was repaid).[39] Any selling shareholder who will be employed by the company going forward should carefully consider the value of the Section 1042 election against the potential benefits to be realized under the ESOP as a participant if the selling shareholder avoids exclusion from the ESOP by forgoing the Section 1042 election.

Prohibition on Allocations to More-Than-25% Shareholders

So long as shares from the 1042 transaction remain in the ESOP, they cannot be allocated to more-than-25% shareholders (i.e., with no time limit). More than 25% means not just more than 25% of the entire company but also more than 25% of any class of stock, more than 25% of the *value* of any class of stock, or more than 25% of any class of stock (or the value of such stock) in a member of the same controlled group of corporations.[40] For purposes of determining the percentage

---

37. Code § 409(n)(1)(A) and (3)(C).

38. Code § 267(c)(4); Treas. Reg. § 1.267(c)-1(a)(4).

39. PLR 9041071 (July 18, 1990).

40. Code § 409(n)(1)(B).

of ownership, one must include stock owned by certain other parties and attributed under Code Section 318(a).[41] These parties include, for example, spouses, children (including legally adopted children), grandchildren, and parents, but other relatives such as grandparents are not included.[42] Additionally, stock allocated to the individual under the ESOP must be counted.[43] (This means that ESOP allocations could push a participant over the 25% threshold and make him or her ineligible for further allocations of shares from the Section 1042 transaction so long as the person is a more-than-25% shareholder.) When determining the percentage of ownership, one must also include stock that can be acquired under options, warrants, or conversion privileges for which there are no conditions that have not been met.[44]

It is important to note that under the attribution rules, someone may be a more-than-25% shareholder even if they are not usually thought of as being a shareholder at all. Thus, if someone owns 30% of the company, a son of that shareholder who works for the company will also be considered a more-than-25% shareholder and thus prohibited from receiving ESOP allocations of stock sold in the Section 1042 transaction. Another example is when someone owns more than 25% of a class of stock (and not necessarily anything close to more than 25% of the entire company) in another company that is a member of the same controlled group. The more-than-25% ownership test is applied to the entire one-year period ending with the date of sale to the ESOP, and also on the date that stock sold in the 1042 sale is allocated to ESOP participants.[45]

---

41. Code § 409(n)(1).
42. Code § 318(a)(1); Treas. Reg. § 1.318-2(b).
43. Code § 318(a)(2)(B)(i) (under Code § 409(n)(1), the employee trust exception in § 318(a)(2)(B)(i) is disregarded). The legislative history to Section 1042 clarifies this refers only to shares allocated to the participant's account (Explanation of Technical Corrections to the Tax Reform Act of 1984 and Other Recent Tax Legislation [Title XVIII of H.R. 3838, 99th Congress, Public 99-514], p. 155).
44. Code Section 318(a)(4), under which someone with an option to acquire stock is treated as owning such stock. The term "option" in Section 318(a)(4) includes warrants and convertible debentures when they are redeemable at the election of the holder. Rev. Ruls. 68-601, 1968-2 C.B. 124, and 89-64, 1989-1 C.B. 91.
45. Code § 409(n)(3)(B).

The Exception for Lineal Descendents of Selling Shareholders

There is an exception to the prohibited allocation rule: a total of 5% of the stock sold in the Section 1042 transaction can be allocated to a seller's lineal descendants.[46] There is no equivalent exception for lineal descendants who are considered more-than-25% shareholders by attribution. Indeed, the IRS has ruled that regardless of the 5% exception, the seller's lineal descendants are still prohibited from receiving allocations if they are more-than-25% shareholders by attribution.[47] This essentially cancels out the lineal descendant exception for many people: since the more-than-25% test is applied to the entire year before the sale, even the lineal descendants of a shareholder who owns 25% or less after the 1042 transaction will be considered more-than-25% shareholders for purposes of this test if the shareholder had more than 25% during the year before the sale. Thus, the lineal descendant exception is very narrow, applying to a seller's children only where the seller holds 25% or less of any class of stock (1) during the year preceding the sale (i.e., where the ESOP already held some stock or where the seller aggregated his or her shares with another seller's shares to reach the 30% threshold for Section 1042) *and* (2) when shares from the Section 1042 transaction are allocated within the ESOP.

Penalties for Violating the Rule

If the prohibited allocation rule is violated, the company sponsoring the ESOP must pay a 50% excise tax on the amount involved, and the person receiving the allocation is currently taxable on the value of the allocation.[48]

Procedural Requirements for the Selling Shareholder

The selling shareholder cannot simply sell to an ESOP and reinvest the proceeds in QRP without further ado. Rather, the seller must meet three procedural requirements:

---

46. Code § 409(n)(3)(A).
47. PLR 9707015 (Nov. 14, 1996).
48. Code § 7979A.

1. The seller must elect Section 1042 treatment in a "statement of election" attached to the seller's tax return.

2. The seller must file with the statement of election a "statement of consent" from the company consenting to the imposition of excise taxes if the ESOP's three-year holding period discussed above is violated or if prohibited allocations are made.

3. The seller must file a notarized "statement of purchase" for each purchase of QRP that is made.

The IRS does not provide official forms for the statement of election, statement of purchase, or statement of consent; taxpayers and practitioners simply read the statute and regulations and follow the rather straightforward requirements set forth there.[49]

Statement of Election

The seller must affirmatively elect Section 1042 treatment in a "statement of election" attached to the seller's income tax return for the taxable year in which the sale occurs, filed on or before the due date (including extensions of time). The 1042 election cannot be revoked once it has been made.[50] The statement of election must describe the securities sold to the ESOP, the date of the sale, the adjusted basis of the securities and the amount realized on the sale, the identity of the ESOP, and, if the sale was part of a single transaction involving other sellers, their names and taxpayer identification numbers and the number of shares they sold.[51]

Statement of Consent

The seller must file with the statement of election a verified statement of consent from the corporation consenting to the imposition of excise taxes on the corporation under Code Sections 4978 (i.e., a 10% tax if the ESOP disposes of the shares from the Section 1042

---

49. For sample forms, see Apton and Coffey, "The Section 1042 Rollover," 137–39.
50. Code § 1042(a)(1), (c)(6); Temp. Treas. Reg. § 1.1042-1T, Q&A-3(a).
51. Temp. Treas. Reg. § 1.1042-1T, Q&A-3(b).

sale within three years) and 4979A (i.e., a 50% tax if a prohibited allocation is made).[52]

Statement of Purchase

For each purchase of QRP (which itself can take place only within the 15-month window of opportunity described above), the seller must execute and have notarized a "statement of purchase" declaring it to be QRP, describing it, and noting its cost and date of purchase. Originally, the IRS required the statement of purchase to be notarized within 30 days, although failure to do this on time might be excused in certain circumstances.[53] The IRS liberalized this requirement in proposed regulatory amendments issued in July 2003: the statement of purchase can be notarized any time not later than the filing of the seller's tax return for the year in which the 1042 sale occurred, or, if the QRP was purchased after that (but within the allowed period), any time not later than the filing of the seller's tax return for the year following the year in which the Section 1042 election was made.[54]

If the seller has already bought the QRP at the time of the 1042 election, the statement of purchase must be attached as part of the statement of election that is filed with the seller's tax return. Otherwise, the statement of purchase must be attached to the seller's income tax return for the year following the year in which the seller elected 1042 treatment.[55]

Consequences of Failing to Comply with the Procedural Requirements

The IRS has stated that failure to comply with procedural requirements for the Section 1042 election is not necessarily fatal where such

---

52. Code §§ 1042(b)(3), 4978(a)-(b), 4979A; Temp. Treas. Reg. § 1.1042-1T, Q&A-2(a)(4), Q&A-3(b).

53. See, e.g., PLR 200019002 (May 12, 2000) (taxpayer's delay excused where it was due to accountant's failure to inform taxpayer of this requirement).

54. REG-121122-03, Internal Revenue Bulletin 2003-37 (September 15, 2003; REG-121122-03 was originally published in the Federal Register on July 10, 2003, 68 Fed.Reg. 41087). REG-121122-03 states that taxpayers can rely on the changed rule for all open tax years pending the issuance of final regulations.

55. Temp. Treas. Reg. § 1.1042-1T, Q&A-3(b)-(c).

requirements appear only in the IRS's regulations and do not go to the essence of the statute. Thus, where sellers have failed to obtain statements of purchase within 30 days of buying QRP (a purely regulatory requirement, which the IRS later moved to change as noted above), the IRS has often ruled that the sellers "substantially complied" with the regulations in those particular circumstances (for example, where the seller had immediately completed a notarized statement of purchase upon learning of the requirement for one, had filed a private letter ruling request, and/or had relied on tax professionals to prepare any necessary forms).[56]

The IRS has also applied this logic in a broader context, as when it ruled that a seller substantially complied with the requirements under Section 1042 where the seller failed to file the statement of election, statement of purchase, and statement of consent with his tax return, but then discovered these requirements and filed an amended return that incorporated these forms.[57] Please note that one is not automatically excused from complying with the Section 1042 requirements in circumstances such as the above, but rather must receive a specific ruling from the IRS pertaining to one's own situation.

Special Situations

There are situations in which shareholders would ordinarily not seem eligible for the Section 1042 "rollover," at least not completely, but in which proper transaction structuring can result in a complete tax deferral under Section 1042.

---

56. See, e.g., PLR 9821022 (Feb. 17, 1998), PLR 9846015 (Aug. 13, 1998), and PLR 9852004 (Sept. 16, 1998), or PLR 200019002, noted above.

57. PLR 9619065 (May 10, 1996). However, compare *Estate of Clause v. Comm.*, 122 T.C. No. 5 (Feb. 9, 2004), in which the U.S. Tax Court held the petitioner, who sold stock to an ESOP in 1996 and purchased QRP within one year of the sale but failed to report it in any way on his tax return for 1996, could not defer recognition of tax under Section 1042 because he failed to file a timely 1042 election and thus failed to elect 1042 treatment. The petitioner in *Clause* filed amended returns (with a statement of election of Section 1042 treatment, a statement of consent from the company, and a statement of purchase of QRP) in 2001, after the IRS had commenced an audit of his 1996 return and mailed the petitioner a notice of deficiency for 1996, but to no avail.

How to Use Seller Financing and Yet Elect Section 1042 Treatment on All the Proceeds

As discussed elsewhere in this book, sellers often finance the ESOP transaction themselves, receiving a note for the amount due. As noted above, the election to defer capital gains taxes under Section 1042 is effective only for the portion of the sale proceeds that is reinvested during the period from 3 months before to 12 months after the sale to the ESOP. This raises a problem for sellers who are financing the sale: If they have no other funds (that is, other than the proceeds from the sale to the ESOP) to invest in QRP, then some of the sale proceeds will likely be paid to them after the 15-month reinvestment period, and they will have to pay capital gains taxes on a portion of the proceeds. The fact that they are receiving the funds years after the sale does not alter this rule.[58]

There is a way out of this dilemma, however: the seller can use what is sometimes called "leveraged QRP"—that is, borrow the funds to reinvest in QRP within the 15-month reinvestment period. One method is to have the QRP serve as collateral for the loan that supplies the funds to purchase it. Investment advisors who have developed this technique use the floating-rate notes mentioned above under the heading "Qualified Replacement Property (QRP)."

How People Who Sell to *Another* Company's ESOP Can Elect Section 1042 Treatment

The most common ESOP issue in mergers and acquisitions is how the shareholder of a non-ESOP company being acquired by an ESOP company can elect the Section 1042 tax deferral for the proceeds of the sale.[59] There is more than one way to do it, but the transaction might be structured somewhat like this: The acquiring company already has an ESOP. The target company sets up an ESOP, which then buys the stock of the target company's shareholder, who elects Section 1042 treatment. (The acquiring company may assist in the financing or even provide financing itself.) The target company's ESOP merges into the

---

58. PLR 8644024 (Aug. 1, 1986).
59. See the chapter in this book on mergers and acquisitions.

acquiring company's ESOP, and the target company itself merges into the acquiring company. This works when either the acquirer or the target is a C corporation. While the Code does not forbid an S corporation to convert to be a C corporation to allow its shareholders to elect Section 1042 deferral and then cause the now-C corporation to merge with an S corporation, the IRS has clearly indicated it would challenge such an arrangement.

Conclusion

The tax deferral under Section 1042 helps make a leveraged sale to an ESOP the ideal business succession strategy for many shareholders of closely held companies. It allows the company to simultaneously defer or eliminate the taxation of the proceeds of the shareholder's sale of his or her shares while creating an ownership plan for the company's employees. When capital gains tax rates are historically low (as was the case after rates were reduced in 2003), Section 1042 becomes relatively less attractive, especially when the QRP might be sold at a point in the future when rates have increased. However, as of 2013, capital gains rates have increased for high-income individuals, which will increase the appeal of Section 1042. The rules for Section 1042 are many and sometimes complex, but, as with other aspects of ESOPs, careful planning with competent legal counsel can smooth over bumps encountered on the road to employee ownership.

Chapter 5

Using ESOPs in Mergers and Acquisitions

William Merten and Vaughn Gordy

ESOPs have long provided an exit strategy for owners of privately held businesses and a platform for management buyouts. Mergers and acquisition (M&A) advisors are increasingly looking to leveraged ESOPs to accomplish both conventional stock and asset acquisitions. This chapter discusses ESOP acquisitions, together with related planning considerations, structures, corporate governance issues, and financing concerns.

General Planning Considerations

Consideration of M&A Opportunities

Considering merger and acquisition opportunities is always a challenge for a company's board of directors, but even more so if the company is partially or wholly owned by an ESOP. While some ESOP company boards do, in fact, receive company purchase offers frequently, the topic of responding to unsolicited offers is complex and certainly beyond the scope of this chapter. This chapter is focused on situations where an ESOP company's board desires to *acquire* a target company or division.

Consideration by the Board of Directors

Acquisition opportunities are usually (but not always) brought to the attention of a company's board by one or more members of its management team. In determining whether the company should offer to purchase another entity, the company's board is legally charged with a responsibility to act in the interest of all shareholders of the company. In undertaking this responsibility, board decisions are generally judged by application of the "business judgment rule," which permits a company's board members to apply their reasonable business judgment in deciding whether to pursue offers (with "business judgment" case law being developed and applied on a state-by-state basis).

Consideration by Trustee(s)

An ESOP trustee is charged with acting solely in the interest of plan participants and beneficiaries and for the exclusive purpose of providing retirement benefits. Given this charge, even in a company that is wholly owned by an ESOP, an ESOP trustee may have slightly different responsibilities than the company's board regarding a company purchase offer. While a board's determination is judged by application of the above-described business judgment rule, the trustee is held to ERISA fiduciary standards.

Transaction Types

Once the decision is made to pursue an acquisition opportunity, the acquisition will generally be structured in one of three ways. As more fully described below, the acquiring company can (1) buy the stock or the assets of the division or company; (2) merge with the division or company; or (3) have the target company or division create a new ESOP, sell itself to the ESOP, and then merge the new ESOP with the acquirer's existing ESOP.

Due Diligence and Key Acquisition Terms

While important, arriving at a price that is agreeable to both parties to an acquisition is usually not the most difficult part of the transaction. Indeed, the time spent negotiating the purchase price will often pale in comparison to the time spent by the purchaser in its completion of thorough due diligence and the time spent by both parties in negotiating escrows, indemnifications, claw-backs, and ongoing executive compensation.

ESOP Trustee Oversight

If an ESOP trustee determines that an acquisition is going to be sizeable (e.g., more than 10% of the acquirer's value), the trustee may request to be involved in the acquisition process. The trustee may want to participate in due diligence and may want to receive an opinion from its independent financial advisor that the acquisition is fair to the ESOP from a financial viewpoint. For larger transactions, the board may want to receive a similar opinion (as to fairness to all shareholders) from its own financial advisor. Although the trustee and the acquirer company will each be concerned with holding down acquisition costs, it is important that the trustee preserve the independence of its financial advisor. It may be appropriate for the acquirer's board to consider having its own financial advisor (i.e., one different from the trustee's advisor).

A company that is partially or wholly owned by an ESOP may have appointed inside employee(s) to serve as ESOP trustee(s). When a major acquisition is in the offing, inside trustee(s) may have conflicts of interest as to one or more aspects of the potential acquisition and thus may have trouble properly fulfilling applicable ERISA fiduciary duties. Should such conflicts arise, consideration should be given to the propriety of appointing either independent trustee(s) or having an independent or an institutional trustee serve as an independent fiduciary who will direct the inside trustee(s) with regard to the acquisition.

Cultural Fit

The acquirer's board will, of course, consider the strategic fit of the target company. It should also consider the cultural fit of the two organizations. Many studies suggest that this cultural fit is the most important contributor to the future success or failure of an acquisition.

Continuation, Termination, or Possible Merger of Existing Target Plans

In almost every M&A transaction, the acquirer will have to consider the disposition of existing (non-ESOP) retirement plans at the target company. The plans can either be (1) continued with amendments, (2) terminated, or (3) merged into the acquirer's existing plans. If they are continued with amendments, basic principles of plan participation, vesting, and retirement will continue to apply. These principles can give rise to various multiple plan issues (e.g., minimum coverage, combined plan limits, or using dividends or distributions to sidestep applicable limits).

If the plans are merged, the acquirer must also review the target plans for possible plan and/or statutory violations. The acquirer does not want existing acquirer plans to become tainted with problems from the target plans.

If a target plan is instead terminated, its participants will become immediately vested and eligible for distributions. This can have the unintended effect of placing considerable sums of money in the hands of financially inexperienced employees (resulting in possible unexpected defections from the target employee workforce).

Finally, a decision must be made about participation by target employees in the acquirer's ESOP. If the acquirer desires to exclude target employees from its ESOP, the exclusion must comply with applicable coverage and/or separate-line-of-business requirements.[1] If, alternatively, the acquirer is prepared to bring target employees into its ESOP, decisions will have to be made regarding timing for participation and service to be counted for eligibility and vesting (with such decisions significantly affecting the acquirer's repurchase obligation, plan benefit levels, and compliance testing).

Valuation Concerns

If the acquirer's use of cash to wholly or partially finance an acquisition has a significant temporary negative effect on the acquirer's cash flow or its ability, e.g., to make necessary capital expenditures, this fact by itself or taken with others (e.g., acquisition-related grants of dilutive stock-based compensation) may lower the per-share value of the acquirer's stock. If it does, the acquirer may decide to amend the plan to provide price protection for certain ESOP participants whose employment may be terminated before the debt can be repaid. If it does, it will also have to determine (1) the length of the protection (e.g., whether it will last for a set period of years or until the acquisition indebtedness is repaid in its entirety), (2) the members of the protected class (e.g., whether the class will include employees who are

---

1. With regard to compliance testing, first see Section 410(b)(6)(c) of the Internal Revenue Code. As to separate lines of businesses, first see Treas. Reg. §1.414(r)-5(d) for the safe harbor for separate lines of business acquired through certain mergers and acquisitions.

terminated due to death, disability, and/or normal retirement), and (3) the terms of the provided protection (e.g., whether the per-share value for the protected class will be determined (a) pursuant to a structured formula, such as one that references the new acquisition indebtedness without actually being tied to it, or (b) without regard to the entirety of the new acquisition indebtedness, but only to the extent necessary to make the post-transaction per-share value at least equal to the per-share transaction price).

As a second valuation concern, it may be appropriate for each company to protect its shareholders by having its own financial advisor. Moreover, if (as described below) the transaction is structured so that an ESOP will exist at each company (even if momentarily), separate trustees and a financial advisor for each ESOP trustee will be *legally required*. While multiple financial advisors can add to a transaction's cost, they may be required depending on the structure and, even if not required, having them may provide the parties (e.g., each company's board of directors) with a requisite degree of comfort.

Use of Retirement Plan and Certain IRA Assets as Transaction Consideration

It is possible, with proper safeguards and adequate disclosure, to use money transferred to the ESOP from a qualified retirement plan (including qualified plan-based IRA dollars transferred into and then from a qualified plan) as consideration in an ESOP acquisition (with any monies rolling into the ESOP from these sources being viewed by senior lender(s) as transaction equity). To the extent that non-*employer* monies will be rolled over to aid in transaction financing, it must be decided how long the rollover opportunity will be extended to plan participants. Federal and state securities laws will also need to be examined for the level of required participant disclosure. Assuming that the amount of *employee* dollars being rolled over comes within federal and state securities law exemption perimeters, a registration statement will not be required. However, even if a registration statement *is not required*, at a minimum an information statement must be prepared to address applicable fraud concerns. Note that while the use of target plan (and/or IRA) monies for transaction financing can often add to the cost and complexity of a transaction, this use does serve to reduce otherwise-required transaction leverage while at the same time providing both an immediate allocation of shares and an immediate company stake to participants directing rollovers.

Use of What Had Been Matching Contributions to Repay Acquisition Indebtedness

Another general consideration when using ESOPs in mergers and acquisitions is whether the company will use what *had been* matching contributions to its 401(k) plan to repay ESOP acquisition indebtedness. Some companies will leave unchanged prior 401(k) cash matching provisions and others will not. Continuing 401(k) matching contributions while making ESOP contributions that are required to service an ESOP loan may result in unintended (and, perhaps, above-market and/or greater-than-base compensation) employee benefit levels. To the extent that such a result does not occur and/or a decision is made to still use what had been cash matching contributions to repay ESOP acquisition indebtedness, a match corresponding to 401(k) salary reduction contributions can, if desired, still be made—and it can be made without additional dollars. A provision can be drafted in the ESOP plan to provide that, instead of allocating suspense account shares under the ESOP in one step (i.e., generally pro-rata based on compensation), suspense account shares will be allocated in a two-step process. First, subject to discrimination testing, an amount of the suspense account shares to be released for the year will be allocated to ESOP participants so as to provide them with a desired benefit level corresponding to a specified percentage of the salary-reduction contributions made under the company's 401(k) plan. The remaining suspense account shares released for the year can then be allocated under the ESOP in a second step—generally, pro-rata based on compensation.

When Section 1042 Treatment Is Desired by Target Shareholders

Advantages

Once a company has adopted a leveraged ESOP, using an ESOP structure to acquire a target company can have significant advantages. First, to the extent that a target shareholder is able to sell his or her company shares to an ESOP and make a Section 1042[2] tax-deferred/tax-free election, the shareholder may be willing to pass on part of his or her income tax savings in the form of a reduced purchase price.

Second, to the extent that IRA and 401(k) dollars are rolled into the ESOP by target company employees, the amount of "outside funds" needed to acquire the target is reduced.

A third advantage is that the notion of providing seller financing will likely be much more attractive to a shareholder selling to an ESOP than it might be in a non-ESOP context. The transaction can be designed so that the seller receives (1) a note from a company to which the seller still exerts a substantial degree of post-transaction control or (2) an ESOP note that is guaranteed by such a company. The transaction can also be designed to permit the seller to obtain a higher subordinated rate of return from a company as to which the seller is inherently familiar. Moreover, assuming that the seller makes a Section 1042 election, the seller can receive cash consideration from the ESOP and then loan any desired amount of seller financing back to the company for the company's use in immediately repaying a like amount of outside (e.g., bank) debt. Such a strategy not only will permit the seller to receive a note from the company rather than the ESOP; it also will provide the seller with a basis in the note equal to the note's face so that the note's *principal* can be received by the seller tax-free. In addition, as is true in almost all ESOP purchase transactions, the transaction's timing can be easily controlled, and the transaction's occurrence can remain totally confidential (e.g., from the target's customers) until the closing of the transaction.

From the *acquirer's* viewpoint, in a C corporation context, both the interest and principal on the related acquisition indebtedness will be effectively tax-deductible. In an S corporation context, it may be possible to acquire a target as a subsidiary of the acquirer and then make a QSUB election so that the target's income will flow up to the acquirer (with the acquirer's income being exempt from federal, and in many cases, state, income tax to the extent it is owned by an ESOP).

---

2.   All section references in this chapter are to the Internal Revenue Code.

Disadvantages

The principal *disadvantage* of using an ESOP to acquire another company is that the transaction structure (as described immediately below) is generally more complicated and may be more costly than a typical asset or stock acquisition structure. A second disadvantage is that the per-share price of the acquirer's ESOP stock value may decrease after the transaction for two reasons. First, as described above, the use of the acquirer's existing cash in the acquisition, either by itself or when coupled with other factors (e.g., grants of stock-based compensation), may possibly lower the per-share value of the company's shares on a post-transaction basis. Second, to the extent that the transaction is structured using the two-step ESOP-merger structure described below, the *per-share* value of the acquirer's stock may decrease due to the increase in the number of outstanding shares following the merger of the two ESOP plans.[3]

Structure

If the acquirer is a C corporation, some practitioners believe that the owner of the target shares can simply exchange his or her shares for shares of the acquirer and then sell received acquirer shares to the acquirer's ESOP (with the former target shareholder thereafter making a Section 1042 election). Because the exchange of shares will be designed to constitute a tax-free reorganization, transaction advisors will have to determine that the tax-free nature of the exchange will not be undermined by an immediate sale of the received shares to the acquirer's ESOP. This will depend in large part on whether the advisors can determine that required reorganization "continuity" is not "busted" by the subsequent sale to the ESOP (with some practitioners believing that continuity still remains since shares are not being sold to the acquirer or a corporation related to the acquirer).[4]

---

3. Whether the increase in the number of outstanding shares will cause the per-share value of the acquirer to so drop will depend in great part on whether the target is acquired at a stock exchange rate that reflects the drop in the target's value resulting from the debt.

4. In this regard, see the continuity of interest regulations at Treas. Reg. §1.368-1(e). See also PLRs 20100528 and 200052023.

If the acquirer is an S corporation (or a C corporation with advisors who believe that continuity is broken by a post-exchange sale to an ESOP), the transaction will likely be structured so that an ESOP that is substantially identical to the acquirer's ESOP is adopted by the target to purchase shares of target shareholder(s). Once target shareholders sell their shares to the target ESOP, with the target ESOP usually using one or more ESOP note(s) for its consideration, the target will generally be merged into the acquirer or an acquirer subsidiary, with the ESOP note(s) received by the target shareholder(s) often being "cashed out" in the merger.[5] The target's ESOP will then be merged into the acquirer's ESOP (with the acquirer assuming the debt obligations of the target ESOP).

Repayment of the acquisition indebtedness will generally occur via the company's cash flow, together with:

1. dollars the target might have annually contributed as a match to its 401(k) plan, with the acquirer, again, having the ability (if desired) to continue under the ESOP any prior 401(k) "match" made by the target and/or the acquirer (with the match, again, being made within the ESOP in the form of company shares), and/or

2. dollars saved due to or because of either (a) ESOP-generated income tax deductions (in a C corporation context) or (b) the ESOP's ownership percentage that goes untaxed in an S corporation.

Administrative and Other Considerations

To the extent that the target is a C corporation that will merge into an S corporation acquirer (or an acquirer QSUB), target stock classes other than common will have to be converted into common before or as a part of the merger. Similarly, any target share class that has voting rights different than those in the S corporation acquirer will have to be converted before or as a part of the merger (because an S corporation can hold only voting and non-voting common shares).

---

5. Note that the cashing out of the ESOP note(s) so received is not an essential step; should the acquirer want to, it can pay the note(s) over time (e.g., through the ESOP), if that is the deal.

To the extent that the acquirer is a C (rather than an S) corporation, an existing multi-class stock structure within either the acquirer or the target may have to be considered when merging the target into the acquirer. In addition, because C corporation ESOP loans generally are shorter than their S corporation counterparts (so as to generate larger deductions that are unnecessary in a 100% S corporation ESOP structure), tracking on a loan-by-loan basis will be required for both the dividend deduction rule of Section 404(k) and the distribution delay rule under Section 409(1)(B), which allows non-death and non-disability distributions to be delayed until the ESOP loan is repaid.

Finally, the share exchange ratio that is applicable in the merger will be the subject of much debate between the respective ESOP trustees and their advisors. For purposes of the exchange, the target may be given quite a low post-ESOP purchase value due to target company obligations on the ESOP note(s) given to the target shareholders. If this is the case, from a financial fairness viewpoint, the target financial advisors may balk at the small number of acquirer shares slated for receipt by target ESOP participants in the merger. If the target is given an equal or *higher* post-ESOP purchase value (with target participants thus slated to receive a *higher* number of shares in the merger), the acquirer will have essentially paid twice for the target: first, by cashing out the target shareholder ESOP note(s) (as a part of the merger), and second, by delivering a not-insignificant amount of acquirer shares in the merger (thereby diluting existing acquirer ESOP participants).

When Section 1042 Treatment Is Not Desired by Target Shareholders

Stock Purchase

Structure

If the acquirer is an S corporation owned wholly by an ESOP, it will not be concerned with deductions. In that case, the target seller can simply sell his or her shares to the acquirer or an acquirer subsidiary. If, on the other hand, the acquirer is a C corporation owned wholly or partially by an ESOP, deductions will be important. In that case, the transaction may be structured so that target shareholders sell their shares to an

ESOP, even if they are not interested in making Section 1042 elections (so that the acquirer-controlled group will have maximized the deductions available to it). Depending upon the view of transaction advisors as to continuity (as discussed above), the target shareholders will either exchange their shares for shares of the acquirer and sell to the acquirer's ESOP, or sell their shares to a newly adopted target ESOP (with the target thereafter merging into the acquirer and the target ESOP thereafter merging into the acquirer's ESOP).

Advantages

If the target shareholder sells shares directly to the acquirer rather than to an ESOP, the advantage will be that Section 404 and Section 415 limits will never become an issue in terms of paying back the acquisition indebtedness. If a target shareholder instead sells shares to an ESOP, all of the normal ESOP advantages will be available. The seller will be able to sell stock rather than assets, which may be preferable in terms of distancing the seller from existing target liabilities. The seller also will receive cash and/or notes rather than shares of another company (as might occur in a typical merger structure). Because the seller will sell shares (rather than assets), the seller also will have a single level of taxation. In addition, because the shares are being sold to an ESOP, the seller will attain capital gains treatment on *all* of his or her sales proceeds, engage (if desired) in a totally confidential transaction, have ESOP-related advantageous seller financing (other than the tax-free receipt of principal) and *not* be asked to take a "haircut" on the price (as he or she might be asked if shares were being sold to the ESOP in a Section 1042 transaction).

From the acquisition company's viewpoint, if the target seller simply sells his or her shares to the acquisition company, both the seller and the acquirer will experience a less complex transaction, and the acquirer will not have to deal with Section 404 and 415 combined plan limits on a post-transaction basis. If, on the other hand, a target shareholder sells to an ESOP (but without making a Section 1042 election), the transaction structure will allow for the use of ESOP rollovers to reduce the amount of transaction-required financing, the use of what had previously been 401(k) matching payments to repay transaction financing, and the deductibility of both interest *and* principal. The extent to which there is a concern with maximizing the acquirer group's deductions will likely turn on whether the acquirer is operating under an S corporation election.

Disadvantages

The principal disadvantage of a target shareholder selling shares but not making a Section 1042 election is that, from the acquirer's viewpoint, the seller has no incentive to take a haircut on his or her sale price. Similarly, seller financing will not be as attractive to the seller, because—without the seller making a Section 1042 election—the transaction cannot be structured so that the seller receives seller-financing principal payments tax-free. To the extent that the target seller instead sells shares directly to the acquirer (rather than to an ESOP), principal payments on the acquisition indebtedness will not be effectively deductible. Moreover, if the acquirer is an S corporation, the seller will have assurance that *all* of his or her gain will be characterized as a capital gain (as would be the case if he or she were to sell shares to an ESOP) *only if* the seller refuses to make a Section 338(h)(10) (asset sale treatment) election.

Administrative (and Other) Considerations

If the target shareholder sells to an ESOP but *does not* make an election under Section 1042, the administrative (and other) considerations described above under "When Section 1042 Treatment Is Desired by Target Shareholders" will apply.

Asset Purchase

Structure

There may be instances in which, for liability, tax, and/or other reasons, the acquirer may want assets purchased rather than stock. Normally, the acquirer would simply purchase assets for itself (i.e., *outside* the context of its ESOP). If, however, all of the acquirer's shares were owned by an ESOP and the acquirer wanted to flow the acquisition indebtedness through the ESOP, an asset purchase structure might be designed in a very limited circumstance to have the acquirer sell treasury shares to the acquirer's ESOP and then use received sale proceeds to purchase all or a portion of the target's ESOP.[6] If the acquirer's ESOP *does not* own 100% of the acquirer's stock, such a structure would likely not be employed since its use would dilute any existing non-ESOP shareholder. In such a case, the target's assets would be sold directly to the acquirer.

Advantages

The principal advantage of an asset sale to the seller is that the seller may be able to get a higher purchase price if the acquirer is a tax-paying C corporation. The reason is that the acquirer will be able to depreciate the purchased assets from their transaction date fair market value (thereby increasing the acquirer's deductions). If all of the acquirer's shares are owned by an ESOP, the acquirer's deductions can be even further increased in such a case if its ability to depreciate the purchased assets at their closing date fair market value is financed by the acquirer's use of treasury share sale proceeds (with the ESOP loan undertaken to permit the ESOP's purchase of treasury shares effectively allowing the acquirer to deduct acquisition indebtedness principal payments).[7]

Of course, to the extent that the acquirer is an S corporation that is wholly owned by an ESOP, deductions will be important to the acquirer group only to the extent they can be taken on applicable state tax returns. In such a case, the principal advantage of an asset purchase structure is that the acquirer may feel that it is acquiring fewer liabilities than it would were it purchasing the target's stock. (Whether this would actually be true would depend on the parties' relative bargaining

---

6. This might occur, for example, if (1) the acquirer was a C corporation that wasn't about to become an S corporation, (2) the acquirer was in need of deductions, (3) it had no outside synthetic equity holders, and (4) it was concerned about moving more ESOP allocations to its newer employees (e.g., in a "have and have nots" scenario).

7. Such additional deductions may not be important if the acquirer can make an election to be taxed as an S corporation. There may, however, be considerations (e.g., desired retention of multiple classes of stock) which make an S corporation election impractical. In addition, even if an S corporation election will be made by a 100% ESOP-owned acquirer, state tax law considerations may make additional deductions desirable.

powers in terms of purchase agreement representation and warranty and indemnification provisions.)

Disadvantages

Again, to the extent that either the acquirer's ESOP does not own 100% of the acquirer's stock or synthetic equity exists outside the ESOP, a structure involving an ESOP's purchase of acquirer treasury shares would be disadvantageous in terms of dilution to non-ESOP acquirer shareholders. From the *seller's* viewpoint, to the extent that assets rather than shares are sold, the seller will have two levels of taxation unless the target has been an S corporation for greater than a fixed number of years[8] (with the first level of taxation being incurred when the target sells the assets and the second level being incurred when the target is liquidated to the seller). A sale of the target's assets rather than its stock will mean that the target's contracts will have to be novated, which may not be required if target shares (rather than target assets) are sold.

Administrative (and Other) Considerations

The administrative and other concerns will be similar to those described above under "When Section 1042 Treatment Is Desired by Target Shareholders," including the possibility of having to track loans and/or dividends.

Acquisition Fiduciary and Settlor Issues

In every acquisition involving one or more ESOPs, normal ESOP acquisition-related fiduciary and settlor issues will arise. The transaction fiduciary will want to assure itself that the company's board is doing its job, and it may be concerned about the possible applicability of a "protected (floor) price" for ESOP shares received by participants prior to the date that new transaction indebtedness is repaid (as discussed above under "Valuation Concerns"). Examples of settlor issues that may arise include (1) an analysis as to whether the target's plans should be amended, terminated, or merged into the acquirer's plans (as discussed above under "Continuation, Termination, or Possible

---

8. The period was five years in 2011 and returned to ten years as of 2012.

Merger of Existing Target Plans"), and (2) decisions as to whether and when target employees will be brought into the acquirer's ESOP (also discussed above under "Continuation, Termination, or Possible Merger of Existing Target Plans").

Acquisition Corporate Governance Issues

Corporate governance issues that arise in acquisitions include the role of the board versus the role of plan fiduciaries and the participant voting process[9] (taking into account concerns regarding possible required pass-through votes and/or rules with regard to shareholder consents).

Acquisition Financing Concerns

Acquisition financing concerns include the added tax advantages of the ESOP term loan and ESOP-related seller financing, which will not be present if conventional financing is used to finance the acquisition of a target. Where an ESOP purchase is included in the acquisition structure, financing-related issues will include (1) a determination of how long the term a new ESOP acquisition indebtedness should be (in terms of its impact on an existing ESOP benefit level and desired deductions, if any), (2) the impact of the acquisition on existing ESOP repurchase obligations, (3) whether participants should be given an opportunity to roll dollars into the ESOP so as to "whittle down" the required amount of ESOP acquisition indebtedness, and (4) whether matching dollars that had previously been contributed to a 401(k) plan should be used to repay ESOP indebtedness (with the match moving inside the ESOP as described above under "Use of What Had Been Matching Contributions to Repay Acquisition Indebtedness").

---

9. There will be a need for a participant vote at the target level if the target has an ESOP and the target will either be merging with the acquirer or selling substantially all of its assets. There will also be a need for a voting pass-through at the acquirer level in the case of a merger unless the merger is designed as a triangular merger (i.e., a merger with a subsidiary of the acquirer rather than the acquirer itself).

Conclusion

The use of an ESOP purchase structure may be advantageous in that a seller who is able to make a Section 1042 election may be willing to pass part of the seller's tax savings on to the acquirer in the form of a reduced purchase price. However, even if a Section 1042 election is *not* made by the seller, an ESOP purchase structure can permit the acquirer to purchase shares with pretax dollars, and it can allow for accessing other qualified plan and IRA monies to reduce the acquisition indebtedness. Monies that would otherwise be contributed as a 401(k) match can also be used under an ESOP purchase structure to provide a partial funding source for periodic loan payments. The factors that make seller financing so attractive under an ESOP purchase structure can also provide the structure with a competitive edge. Coupling these advantages with the manner in which ESOP financing enhances cash flow (which can be used for both debt reduction and periodic growth) may, in fact, make the ESOP structure a worthy alternative to traditional M&A acquisition structures in many situations. An ESOP purchase structure can also serve as a go-forward investment and/or acquisition platform. Finally, the use of an ESOP as a stalking horse and/or acquisition tool may also provide an acquirer or an M&A firm with advantage(s) not found elsewhere.

With proper planning, the considerations that have to be explored and quantified in any ESOP structure need not become structural drawbacks. In an economy in which M&A advisors and private equity groups are looking for flexible structures they can use to take an acquisition to completion, the leveraged ESOP purchase structure presents a compelling alternative. Although beyond the scope of this chapter, the structure's use may also make an ESOP an appropriate acquisition vehicle in the case of a desired divestiture (including a spinoff of a division or company, e.g., a failed "roll-up" company) and/or a private equity group that is seeking to liquidate its equity investment in a "sideways" company.

Part 2
Financing

Chapter 6

The Changing Faces of ESOP Financing

Mary Josephs

"Show me the money!" This famous line from the movie *Jerry Maguire* says it all. Cash at close is an important—and sometimes key—consideration in both assessing the feasibility of an ESOP and creating the optimal structure for a particular seller or company. So where is the money? For years the banker's answer has been, "it depends." This noncommittal answer is not intended to dodge the question or create mystery. "It depends" was the right answer decades ago and is even truer today.

In the earlier years of ESOPs, some factors were different than they are now:

* Only C corporations could have their stock owned by an ESOP.

* Capital gains tax rates were high.

* Lending rates were high (generally being based on prime until the early 1990s).

* There were fewer global commercial banks and many more "community" banks than we have today.

Because of the then high-capital gains rates, many ESOP transactions had a Section 1042 capital gains component. With the exception of a select group of high-profile and anti-takeover deals in the 1980s and early 1990s, many ESOPs were formed in smaller middle-market companies that used their local community banks. The predominant financing structure was fully secured credit, often with a personal guarantee. If the assets of the company were insufficient collateral, it was not unusual for sellers to pledge the Section 1042 qualified replacement property (see the chapter in this book on Section 1042 for more detail) as collateral. It was also typical to use a "staged" approach to ESOP ownership. Owners often began with a 30% ESOP, the minimum requirement to enjoy the Section 1042 tax deferral. And when they had the debt capacity to look at an additional event, they did so.

In summary, in the 1980s and 1990s, ESOPs were generally financed as single-bank deals, fully secured by company collateral (sometimes with personal guarantees) and /or the Section 1042 replacement properties. Whether the selling shareholder could secure proceeds "free and clear" of encumbrances often depended on the collateral associated with the transaction.

The environment for ESOPs changed greatly in subsequent years:

- An S corporation can have its stock owned by an ESOP.

- The ESOP as an S corporation shareholder does not pay federal income taxes (employees will pay tax when they receive distributions in the future).

- Privately held businesses are more likely than before to be S corporations or LLCs rather than C corporations.

- Interest rates are at a historic low, with LIBOR under 1%.

- Many top-performing American businesses are service businesses, where employees are key assets and companies have minimal natural tax shields (i.e., depreciation).

- Bank markets have become significantly more creative and competitive, even for middle-market companies.

- Non-bank financial institutions bear investigation as a source of funds that barely existed before 2000.

- The unique financing needs of mature ESOP companies and of certain other private companies have led markets to create forms of appropriately priced "patient" capital.

- The use of Section 1042 qualified replacement property as collateral is less frequent. Sellers now tend to do smaller deals, avoid electing Section 1042 treatment, or use seller financing.

- There is less use of personal guarantees as part of an ESOP structure.

- There has been significantly less use of the Section 1042 tax deferral due to historically low capital gains rates, especially between 1997 and 2012, plus the popularity of S corporation ESOPs (where Section 1042 is not available).

- Increasingly, using seller financing or a smaller transaction size can replace third-party mezzanine financing.

- Increasingly, extreme care may be given to the overall benefit plan design to help ensure the long-term capital sustainability of the ESOP company.

ESOPs are a capital market alternative

ESOPs are retirement plans governed by ERISA under the regulatory oversight of the U.S. Department of Labor and Internal Revenue Service. However, from a seller's perspective, ESOPs are a capital markets alternative. While it is critical to be cognizant of the legal rules for ESOPs, the capital market and corporate finance components of ESOP transactions are both highly dynamic and incredibly important. A business owner chooses an ESOP because, from a corporate finance and strategic alternatives perspective, it optimally meets his or her objectives. Obtaining liquidity at close and over time is an important objective. As the following chapters discuss, access to capital has become significantly more complex in recent years. There are more providers, more types of capital, and more capital structures to choose from. The price and terms of each of these change dynamically. It is important to stay open-minded, knowledgeable, and aware of the selling owner's objectives. This will guide you to the right questions at the right time, understanding the tradeoffs and the optimal balance for any given transaction.

Chapter 7

ESOP Underwriting Considerations

Mary Josephs and Neal Hawkins

This chapter focuses on the general and unique underwriting considerations of ESOP transactions, providing a guide for lenders, borrowers, and service providers. Some of these considerations are typical in any credit transaction but are described here to provide a clear understanding of the complete underwriting of an ESOP company. In general terms, the underwriting process involves providing quantitative and qualitative information for a lender or investor to price an adequate return in exchange for the risk of a transaction.

Unique Underwriting Considerations

On one hand, leveraged ESOPs do not differ significantly from other applications for term debt: the lender needs to evaluate the borrower's debt capacity for supporting the proposed credit. However, the unique characteristics of ESOPs, such as those detailed below, contribute to common underwriting confusion.

Purpose

The lender must understand all the varying objectives of a particular transaction. The transaction structure can differ depending on the underlying objectives. Examples of different applications for leveraged ESOPs include:

• *Nonproductive Debt:*
   1. Achieving full or partial liquidity for a closely held business owner through the owner selling existing shares to the ESOP.

2. Second-stage ESOP transactions.

3. Attaining liquidity on a tax-advantaged basis, using Section 1042 securities for deferral of capital gains on the sale.

4. Facilitating an MBO (management buyout).

5. Public-to-private transactions.

6. Corporate spinoffs.

7. Achieving full or partial liquidity for a closely held business owner through the company issuing new shares of stock, selling those shares to the ESOP, and using the cash proceeds to provide liquidity to the owner.

- *Productive Debt:*

1. Refinancing existing debt on a tax-advantaged basis with debt repayments "above the line" (see "Employee Benefit Expense" below).

2. Issuing new debt on a tax-advantaged basis with debt repayments "above the line."

3. Refinancing higher-priced debt from an existing transaction, such as mezzanine financing or seller notes.

4. Making an acquisition.

productive v. nonproductive debt

Depending on the purpose of the leveraged ESOP, the debt can be considered "productive" or "nonproductive." Generally, productive debt adds debt to a balance sheet with a corresponding asset addition. The incremental debt is used to purchase an asset or assets that produce incremental cash flow for the company. Ideally, the cash flow generated from the asset purchase is more than sufficient to service the incremental debt. In addition to the incremental cash flow, the asset itself will have collateral loan value to the lender. The incremental cash flow and loan value of the asset both enhance the proposed senior credit underwriting.

With nonproductive debt, a liability is added to the balance sheet without a corresponding addition of income-producing hard assets. "Soft" issues such as a projected increase in margins attributable to employee ownership are difficult for a lender to underwrite. On the

productive debt adds an asset to the balance sheet

other hand, add-backs of nonrecurring historical expenses such as the owner's salary and historical employee benefit expenses are considered in the underwriting process. Ideally, the debt is serviced with the existing asset base and existing cash flow plus "add-backs" (see "Cash Flow Available for Debt Service" below for further explanation of add-backs).

For example, new shares of stock can be issued to facilitate tax-advantaged financing. Both the existing shareholders and the company need to take into account the impact of dilution on share value when using this strategy. For example, if a company has an enterprise value of $20 million and 200 shares of stock outstanding, the value per share is $100,000. If this company were to issue 50 new shares of stock, each share would then be worth only $80,000 ($20 million ÷ 250 shares). The 50 new shares are worth $4 million (50 shares × $80,000 per share). However, the preexisting 200 shares are only worth $16 million (200 shares × $80,000 per share). Presuming the company was using this $4 million to refinance existing non-ESOP debt, there could be a $1,600,000 tax shield ($4 million × 40% tax rate) created to partially offset the negative impact of dilution.

Security/Collateral

A major component in determining the risk of a loan is to evaluate any secondary sources of repayment, such as a security interest in company assets, personal guarantees, or a pledge of securities. A company that would have sufficient assets or collateral to cover a loan obligation would be viewed as a safer investment than a comparable company with limited asset support.

A senior lender will look at the balance sheet assets such as receivables, raw materials, finished goods, property, plants, or equipment and apply applicable advance rates against those assets to derive a "borrowing base." The borrowing base, described in more detail below, is a calculation to determine the asset coverage of a borrower, which is one data point a lender uses in calculating the risk associated with a loan.

If the asset coverage is not sufficient to cover the loan, also known as an "air ball" or a "collateral shortfall" (common in service businesses), the lender can either (1) gain comfort in the cash flows to repay the loan (see under "Cash Flow Loan in chapter 9"), (2) request a guarantee from

air ball/collateral shortfall

the selling shareholder(s) and/or management, and/or (3) request a pledge back of 1042 securities (see under "Section 1042 Benefit" below).

Below is a description of the different assets a lender will review along with a general "rule of thumb" advance rate:

- *Eligible Accounts Receivable: 80%.* If the company sells solely to top-credit quality customers with nominal bad debt experience, a higher advance rate may be warranted. Similarly, if the company has significant account dilution and/or write-offs, the advance rate on accounts receivable may be less than 80%. Eligibility criteria typically exclude from the borrowing base inter-company and related party receivables, foreign receivables, receivables over 90 days past due, and so on.

- *Eligible Inventory: 50%.* If raw materials or finished goods inventory consist of a commodity, such as paper, steel, cocoa beans, and so on, higher advance rates may be warranted. High perishability and obsolescence or lack of marketability may negatively affect the advance rates. Work in process is almost always considered ineligible. Eligibility of finished goods varies from company to company. To the extent finished goods are highly proprietary to a particular customer, with limited alternative applications, advance rates will be low to nothing. Lastly, in asset-based transactions, the lender may cap inventory borrowings regardless of what the borrowing base may suggest.

- *Real Estate: 0% to 70%.* First, the lender and company will have to resolve all environmental issues, regardless of whether the lender is actually taking a mortgage on the property. The market value will be ascertained from a third-party appraiser hired by the lender. The loan value of the real estate is usually 70% of the market value less 100% of any existing liens and encumbrances. It is unusual to have a more aggressive advance than 70%. Factors that would influence a smaller advance include limited alternative uses for the facility, poor geographic location of the facility, and perceived environmental risks of the facility.

- *Fixed Assets: 50% of book value.* 50% of book value is a good rule of thumb. However, if a lender is truly relying on the fixed assets of a particular company, an independent appraisal from a third party is solicited. Advance rates on the appraised value are typically 75% of orderly liquidation value or 90% of "under the hammer" or "fire sale" liquidation. The fixed asset appraisal will, as with the real estate appraisal, need to be performed by an independent third party hired by the lender.

Borrowing Base Certificate

The exact form of a borrowing base certificate will vary from lender to lender. The concept, nonetheless, is similar—to evidence at regular intervals (anywhere from daily to quarterly depending on the loan structure) the loan value of the assets. The lender then compares the loan value of the assets with the credit outstanding at that same time. The borrowing base certificate is the means by which the lender limits total credit outstanding and ensures the borrower cannot borrow in excess of the proposed collateral structure. A borrower is "capped," unable to borrow in excess of the limits of its borrowing base certificate. In the example in table 7-1, the borrowing base certificate restricts the company's total borrowings to $10.5 million. Because the borrower already has $10 million outstanding under the line, it can borrow only an additional $500,000 at this point.

Table 7-1. Basic Borrowing Base Certificate for Current Assets			
Asset	**Gross value**	**Advance rate**	**Loan value**
Accounts receivable	$10,000,000	80%	$8,000,000
Inventory	$5,000,000	50%	2,500,000
Eligible borrowing base			$10,500,000
Less: revolving line of credit outstanding			(10,000,000)
Amount available to be drawn under the $12,000,000 line of credit			$500,000

Collateral Shortfall or Air Ball

The ESOP credit request often results in a collateral shortfall. The loan value of the assets is insufficient to cover the basic borrowing needs of the company and the ESOP debt.

As table 7-2 illustrates, the ESOP debt request can create a shortfall in asset coverage. Resolving this shortfall issue is the part of the art of structuring the ESOP transaction. (See "Overcoming Common

Underwriting Obstacles" below for a discussion of how to cover a collateral shortfall.)

Table 7-2. Example of an ESOP Term Loan Creating a Collateral Shortfall

Asset	Gross value	Advance rate	Loan value
Accounts receivable	$10,000,000	80%	$8,000,000
Inventory	$5,000,000	50%	2,500,000
Real estate	$5,000,000	70%	3,500,000
Fixed assets	$8,000,000	50%	4,000,000
Total loan value of collateral			$18,000,000
Less: existing revolver and term debt requirements			(10,000,000)
Collateral available for ESOP term loan			$8,000,000
Less: ESOP term loan			(20,000,000)
Collateral shortfall			$(12,000,000)

Section 1042 Benefit

Under Section 1042 of the Internal Revenue Code (the "Code"), when shares of a C corporation are sold to an ESOT (employee stock ownership trust) that owns 30% or more of the company, the seller can defer the capital gains tax obligation on proceeds from that sale so long as the seller reinvests proceeds in "qualified replacement property." It is advisable to consult a professional specializing in Section 1042 investment requirements to ensure proper investment of sales proceeds. In general, "qualified replacement property" includes stocks and bonds of domestic corporations. This advantageous tax treatment of Section 1042 for the selling shareholder is an important incentive for a seller to consider selling to the employees. Section 1042 also provides an asset that is very attractive collateral to lenders: cash. Section 1042 securities can be considered the "asset of last resort" in terms of a seller's willingness to pledge. While it may be discouraging to some sellers to pledge Section 1042 securities, it is important to recognize the benefits to the seller of selling to an ESOP, including, among other things:

1. Gaining liquidity, and with less financial burden on the company than non-ESOP debt

2. Diversifying assets

3. Deferring capital gains

4. Opportunities for estate planning

5. Enabling an ownership transition

6. Increased flexibility in work schedule if desired

7. Continued involvement if desired

8. Creating employee ownership

Pledging some or all of the Section 1042 proceeds may be a reasonable price to pay in the short run to achieve the seller's long-term objectives. For example, table 7-3 assumes a $10 million sale regardless if the sale is to a third party or an ESOP. There is a $1.5 million cash advantage to the seller if the ESOP is chosen as the sales vehicle.

Table 7-3. Seller's Section 1042 Benefit		
	Non-ESOP	ESOP
Sales proceeds	$10,000,000	$10,000,000
Capital gains tax (15%)	(1,500,000)	N/A
Net proceeds to seller	$8,500,000	$10,000,000

1042 Securities as Collateral

Having the 1042 replacement securities serve as collateral is by no means a given in every ESOP transaction. However, in the event that Section 1042 is the full or partial solution to a collateral shortfall (see table 7-2 above for an example of a $12 million shortfall), the following issues should be considered.

Advance Rate on 1042 Assets

Advance rates for marketable securities vary depending on the perceived riskiness of the security. Table 7-4 gives typical margin guidelines for lenders. Lenders require an advance rate, or "margin" to provide a cushion for both marketability of the security and the inevitable valuation fluctuations.

If a lender were to strictly adhere to the advance rates in table 7-4, a seller would actually need to post collateral plus the margin "cushion." For example, if the seller invested rollover proceeds in a New York Stock Exchange stock portfolio, technically, for the seller to completely cover a $12 million collateral shortfall on a fully margined basis, the seller would need to pledge $17.1 million ($12 million divided by .7) in collateral.

Table 7-4. Margin Requirements for Lenders: Advance Rates for Marketable Securities

Marketable security pledged	Advance rate on security
Listed stock	70%
Corporate bonds: maturity of five years or less	85%
Corporate bonds: maturity of more than five years	80%

Release Provisions for 1042 Assets

Release provisions for Section 1042 assets (i.e., the seller's qualified replacement property) held as collateral can be important to the seller. On the most conservative side, Section 1042 assets would be pledged on a fully margined basis up front and then released pro rata as the loan is paid down. Other ideas include:

• Structuring the ESOP loan to not require Section 1042 qualified replacement property to be in margin initially, and commencing the release of Section 1042 qualified replacement property from collateral once the loan is in margin and the loan value of the collateral (the value of the securities times the advance rate) equals the principal outstanding.

• Accelerating the release of qualified replacement property from collateral as leverage (the ratio of funded debt to EBITDAE) decreases. For example, a loan that may need to be fully secured when the leverage is 4:1 can release qualified replacement property from collateral when leverage falls below 2:1.

• Releasing qualified replacement property from collateral if the company achieves certain minimum EBITDAE levels. This strategy is particularly helpful in a transaction where cash flow projections are significantly improved from historical cash flows. In a sense, the seller "underwrites" the promised improvements. When the improvements are realized, the collateral is released.

- "Sharing" of the release. In situations where the initial credit structure includes a partial pledge of Section 1042 assets and a portion of unsecured credit exposure, the lender may want to be in a fully margined position before the release of the seller's pledge. This could conflict with the seller's objectives to accelerate the release of his or her collateral pledge. A compromise structure allows a partial release of qualified replacement property from collateral for each dollar of principal reduction. For example, for every dollar of principal reduction, the lender could release 50 cents of securities held as collateral.

- The seller often successfully negotiates the retention of interest earned on the qualified replacement property so long as the principal amount of the securities stays within the required margin.

- Distribution of asset appreciation is also a point of negotiation. As long as there are no defaults in the loan agreement and no financial deterioration in the portfolio held as collateral, the seller can negotiate to have any appreciation in the account swept out of the "collateral" account and into an unpledged account on a regular basis.

Typical Terms and Conditions for ESOP Loans

Borrower

ESOP loans are preferably made directly to the company, not to the ESOT itself. This way, the lender makes a loan directly to the ultimate source of repayment. It is possible to loan to the ESOT with a guarantee from the company. This is certainly considered in situations where there are structuring obstacles to lending directly to the company (for example, where push-down accounting is to be avoided, where the loan is secured by Section 1042 assets, or where there are regulatory issues). Figure 7-1 shows the funds flow for a loan directly to the company. Figure 7-2 details the funds flow for a loan to the ESOP trust with a collateralized guarantee from the company.

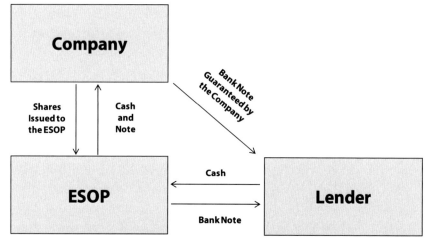

Figure 7-1. Funds flow for a loan directly to the company

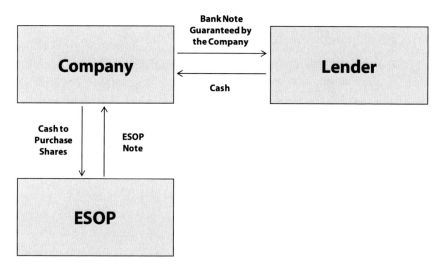

Figure 7-2. Funds flow for a loan to the ESOP trust with a collateralized guarantee from the company

Credit Facilities

Generally, lenders will structure the revolving line of credit as a separate credit facility from term debt. Theoretically, the revolving line of credit should be secured by the current assets of the company supporting the short-term working capital borrowings. The term debt is then secured by the fixed (long-term) assets of a company. Real estate loans are often structured as separate loans as well. With an ESOP loan, there are usually at least two credit facilities, a working capital revolving credit facility, and an ESOP term loan. There could be a third or fourth facility for real estate or other term debt. Sometimes lenders structure the undersecured or cash flow portion of the term loan as a separate credit facility with a different interest rate and amortization structure than the fully secured facilities. Chapter 9 provides more information on the different types of capital.

Facility A: Working Capital Revolving Credit Facility

It is imperative that the lender consider all borrowing needs of the company in conjunction with the ESOP. A lender generally prefers to have long-term debt secured by the long-term assets and current debt secured by the current assets. With a strong company that has historically self-financed its working capital needs, there can be an "overcollateralized" position with respect to current assets covering revolver needs and an "undercollateralized" position with respect to long-term assets covering term debt needs. In this situation, some lenders will find it acceptable to secure all or part of the ESOP term debt with current assets. This can be done formally with a "block" on the borrowing base as illustrated by table 7-5, or informally with a minimum availability covenant. With the BBC (borrowing base certificate) in table 7-5, a "block" would be executed for a company with a $13 million current asset loan value and revolver needs that are never projected to exceed $9 million.

Table 7-5. Borrowing Base Certificate Using Short-Term Assets to "Cover" Collateral Needs for Term Loan

	Eligible asset value	Advance rate	Loan value of asset
Accounts receivable	$10,000,000	80%	$8,000,000
Inventory	$10,000,000	50%	5,000,000
Total available for borrowing			$13,000,000
Less: "block" for term loan collateral			(4,000,000)
Total available for revolver borrowing			$9,000,000

In this example, the first $4 million of availability would always be used to support the term loans outstanding, reducing the revolver availability.

Facility B: ESOP Term Loan

Current market conditions price term debt similar to revolving debt, particularly when they are both multi-year facilities, cross-collateralized and cross-defaulted.

Amortization

The amortization period is typically five to seven years, depending on structure and debt service ability. Fully secured loans can sustain a longer amortization schedule than cash flow loans. Cash flow loans are required to be amortized over five years to seven years. Since Code Section 133 (which provided a tax incentive for ESOP lenders) was repealed in 1996, lenders have no longer been concerned about exact mirror loan provisions under which the principal repayments on ESOP loans mirror the benefit allocation. Therefore, a borrower can, with after-tax cash flow, repay the bank debt faster than the actual benefits are allocated.

Rate

The rate varies depending on leverage and debt service coverage. LIBOR (London Inter-Bank Offer Rate) is a common pricing benchmark as an alternative to prime. It is common for lenders to propose a pricing grid that commits to price reductions as the leverage decreases due to either debt repayment and/or earnings increases (table 7-6). In down markets, some banks may enforce an interest rate floor.

Table 7-6. Example Performance Pricing Matrix	
Cash flow leverage ratio	Loan pricing spread over LIBOR
Greater than 3.25:1	300
Between 3.00 and 3.25:1	250
Between 2.50 and 3.00:1	225
Between 2.00 and 2.50:1	200
Less than 2.00:1	175

Closing Fee

Commitment fees range from .5% to 3.0% on ESOP accommodations. Factors that warrant the higher end of the fee range include highly leveraged transactions; highly complex transactions; syndicated and/ or underwritten transactions where the lender assumes the syndication risk; and cash flow-based, substantially undersecured transactions. Factors that warrant the lower end of the fee range include lower leverage, ample collateral, and highly competitive situations.

Non-use Fee

A facility fee ranging from 1/8% to .75% is charged on the unused portion of line commitments. This fee compensates the lender for reserves (direct costs to the lender) that must be held on commitments upon which there are no borrowings (revenues to lender to offset costs). One strategy to reduce non-use fees is to structure the line with seasonal increases as needed, minimizing the unused commitment.

Basic Underwriting Guidelines

Management Team

Although management is an important factor in every credit situation, the issue is even more pertinent with ESOPs. If the founder is selling out or just backing out, the lender will need to be confident that the replacement management team can continue to generate the earnings level that the lender is underwriting. The lender will also want to understand the experience the management team has with indebtedness and achieving covenants on a quarterly basis. In addition, a lender will want to understand the impact of any key individuals who would be departing, because they may retain valuable information or key relationships that could affect the business going forward. As part of the transaction, a trustee may require certain key individuals to sign employment agreements covering a given period, which may help decrease any management risk to the lender. For management employees, a succession plan and timeline will also help to decrease the risk for a lender.

Cash Flow Available for Debt Service

Cash flow available for debt service is a critical underwriting concept for all credit. The lender needs to feel comfortable the company has sufficient cash flow to service the proposed credit request. A common benchmark to determine debt service is EBITDA (earnings before interest, taxes, depreciation, and amortization). Lenders must consider what other claims exist on cash flow in addition to debt service. Examples include required maintenance and capital expenditures, lease payments, and other fixed charges. With a retailer, for example, the company has substantial capital expenditures each year to keep the stores updated. If the company does not make certain capital expenditures, its business will suffer.

Therefore, a more prudent calculation of cash flow available for debt service is EBITDA less (1) required capital expenditures for ongoing operations, (2) required cash flow to service other non-ESOP debt, and (3) other necessary claims on cash flow for a particular company and industry. With ESOPs, to determine cash flow available for debt service, simply add "add-backs" to the result of the above. Common add-backs of nonrecurring historical expenses include:

- salary and other compensation attributable to a departing shareholder;

- compensation reductions contemplated as a result of the transaction;

- other expenses related to the owner that the company will not cover going forward;

- historical 401(k) matching and profit sharing expenses to the extent the previous employee benefit will be replaced by the ESOP benefit; and

- historical losses from nonrecurring events.

The example in table 7-7 demonstrates the significance of the above variables in determining cash flow available for ESOP debt service. The preexisting requirements for cash flow such as required capital expenditures and existing debt service cannot be ignored. However, add-backs and other adjustments from nonrecurring expenses can offset their impact on cash flow available for debt service.

Table 7-7. Cash Flow Available for Debt Service	
EBITDA	$2,000,000
Less: required capital expenditures	(500,000)
P&L for existing debt	(500,000)
EBITDA available for new debt service	$1,000,000
Plus: departing owner's salary	600,000
Historical employee benefit expense	200,000
Nonrecurring legal expenses	250,000
EBITDAE available for ESOP debt	$2,050,000

Modeling the Tax Shield to Assess Net Cash Flow Available for Debt Service and Fixed Charge Coverage Ratios

C Corporations

For a C corporation, the maximum tax shield for the ESOP debt (non-ESOP debt has no tax shield) is 25% of covered payroll. A company may exceed this limitation by issuing a "reasonable" dividend (typically 10%–15% of value) "above the line." However,

1. The maximum allowable dividend cannot exceed the "reasonable" standard. Therefore, in many cases it is impossible to truly drive taxes to zero.

2. The company must allocate a comparable amount of stock to the participants' accounts. By overaccelerating the stock contribution, the company could be inadvertently creating a human resource issue for newer employees, who will not have the opportunity to participate as much as they had intended.

3. The dividend is a preference item for purposes of calculating the alternative minimum tax (AMT). Thus, a company still may not achieve a reduced tax rate.

4. The dividend could be paid on all shares. Unless the ESOP holds a separate class of stock (acceptable only for C corporations) or

owns 100% of the company, cash intended for debt service could inadvertently flow to non-ESOP shareholders.

Precision is imperative in calculating the true tax shield in order to avoid overstating projected cash flow in the underwriting.

S Corporations

For an S corporation, allocations must be made using the principal-and-interest method, thus exhausting the 25% cap more quickly. Once again, it is important to avoid inadvertently overstating cash flow available for debt service by misrepresenting the tax shield. Implications are different for 100% ESOP-owned S corporations and partially ESOP-owned S corporations.

For a partially ESOP-owned S corporation, the non-ESOP shareholder will be required to pay taxes on its percentage of income earned. Typically, an S corporation dividends (in S corporation terms, "distributes") to the owner the amount needed to pay taxes. Because there can be only one class of stock in an S corporation, a pro-rata cash dividend must also go to the ESOP. Because the ESOP does not have a tax obligation, the ESOP can either (1) keep the cash in the plan to fund future acquisitions or for repurchase obligation protection, or (2) dividend (prepay the internal loan) the cash back to the company.

Employee Benefit Expense

With leveraged ESOPs, to the extent the company is allocating shares to participants' accounts (subject to Code Section 415 and other restrictions that cap the maximum amount of employee benefits a company is able to expense), the repayment of debt can be "expensed." Debt can be repaid "above the line" instead of with after-tax cash flow. This "tax shield" related to ESOP debt makes ESOP debt significantly less expensive than other forms of debt (table 7-8).

In this example, the repayment of a similar $1 million loan payment saves the company $400,000 in taxes when paid as an ESOP loan versus a non-ESOP loan. If there were a $10,000,000 loan, the total tax shield over the term of the loan would be $4,000,000 ($400,000 tax shield per $1,000,000 × $10,000,000).

Table 7-8. ESOP Tax Savings Example		
	Non-ESOP loan	ESOP loan
Operating profit	$2,000,000	$2,000,000
ESOP payment	(0)	(1,000,000)
Pretax income	$2,000,000	$1,000,000
Taxes (40%)	(800,000)	(400,000)
Net profit	$1,200,000	$ 600,000
Loan payment	(1,000,000)	N/A
Net cash	$ 200,000	$ 600,000

Accounting Treatment

The stock bought in a leveraged ESOP is held, like treasury stock, in a contra-equity account until it is allocated to participants' accounts as the loan is paid off. This can create a negative tangible net worth and solvency issues. For example, in table 7-9, the company's equity declines from $6 million to negative $1 million as a result of accounting for the ESOP transaction.

Table 7-9. Negative Net Worth Example			
	Pre-ESOP	ESOP	Post-ESOP
Assets	$10,000,000	$0	$10,000,000
Liabilities	(4,000,000)	(7,000,000)	(11,000,000)
Equity	$6,000,000	$(7,000,000)	$(1,000,000)
Leverage	.67x	N/A	$11,000,000 ÷ $(1,000,000)

Factoring the Repurchase Obligation into the Cash Flow Available for Debt Service

In closely held companies, ESOP shares have a mandatory put option allowing vested participants who leave the company to put distributed shares back to the sponsor company in exchange for the current fair market value of the stock (based on an annual valuation of the ESOP shares). The company has the obligation to buy back those shares in a manner consistent with plan documents. (Note that distributions of leveraged shares generally may be deferred until the loan that bought those shares is repaid.) In first-time ESOP transactions that do not use a rollover of other plan assets as a source of equity, the shares have not generally been allocated and/or vested sufficiently to cause concern with any material accumulation of unforeseen expenses. The deferral of the put option (but for death, disability, and retirement) gives the lender further comfort that the repurchase obligation will not cause an unforeseen drain on cash flow.

In second-stage transactions, mature employee-owned companies, and transactions where a rollover of existing plan assets serves as a source of funds for the transaction, lenders need to project repurchase obligations into the cash flow analysis. Some companies develop their own models because they truly have a good sense of retirement patterns. Larger companies use one of a few software products that have actuarially based models to aid in forecasting. The repurchase obligation, though not required by GAAP to be listed on the balance sheet, is a real pre-cash-flow, available-for-debt-service obligation of the company, and it must be considered in subsequent years of all ESOP transactions.

A lender cannot possibly have an accurate account of cash flow available for debt service without accurately modeling both the tax shield and the repurchase obligation.

Solvency

In a leveraged ESOP transaction, stock purchased by the ESOP is held as treasury stock until released gradually into plan participants' accounts, often resulting in negative total net worth. Notwithstanding other issues affecting solvency, this "accounting" issue is typically addressed through the signing of a "solvency affidavit." With this affidavit, counsel has advised that the bank is protected from fraudulent conveyance issues. In highly structured multi-investor transactions, bank lenders have asked to receive a solvency opinion or to be permitted to rely on the solvency opinion rendered to the trustee.

Solvency Opinion

In highly leveraged and 100% S corporation ESOP transactions, trustees increasingly ask for a solvency opinion from an independent valuation firm. Lenders may receive a copy of the solvency opinion whenever it is a trustee's requirement, and in some situations they ask to rely upon the same solvency opinion.

Covenants

Covenants are part of nearly every loan agreement. However, some of the lender's favorite covenants, minimum tangible net worth and maximum leverage (total liabilities to tangible net worth), lose their efficacy in light of the contra-equity accounting in leveraged ESOPs. Lenders need to focus instead on:

- Cash flow, as defined by minimum EBITDAE (earnings before interest, taxes, depreciation, amortization, and employee benefits expense). This benchmark is set to ensure the company meets minimum earning thresholds to service debt.

- The debt service coverage ratio, which is defined as the ratio of EBITDAE to all required principal and interest payments. The benchmark will vary depending on the deal structure. For example, fully secured credits may require 1:1 coverage whereas a "cash flow" structure may require 1:2 or greater coverage.

- Leverage, which is more effectively defined as senior debt to EBITDAE in ESOP transactions.

- Interest coverage (EBITDAE/interest expense) and fixed charge coverage (EBITDAE/fixed charges) ratios also are helpful in monitoring the financial leverage and debt service capability of the company.

Working with Experienced Service Providers

With ESOP transactions, it is important to have confidence in each of the parties to the transaction. The lender is underwriting its customer, the company. However, with ESOPs, a lender should also evaluate the financial advisor, trustee, plan administrator, and legal counsel. Though it would be unusual for the senior lender to be liable in the event of plan disqualification, plan disqualification does have significant cash flow implications that could affect a company's ability to meet the proposed debt service requirements. For example, if a plan with a $10 million loan were disqualified, the loan would have to be repaid with after-tax dollars, much like any other non-ESOP corporate debt. This would increase the cash flow required to service the debt by approximately $4 million, assuming a 40% corporate tax rate.

Conditions Precedent

Because of the complexities of the ESOP, certain other conditions are likely to be required that are not part of a non-ESOP loan. For example:

- *Acceptable valuation firm:* The lender will want to ensure that the "adequate consideration" opinion is provided by an independent, experienced, and reputable firm.

- *Acceptable trustee:* Many transactions employ outside fiduciaries to represent the buyer, the ESOT. The lender will want to verify the independence and prudence of whoever is serving as the trustee.

- *Acceptable and independent counsel representing the ESOT:* It is advisable that experienced ESOP counsel represent the trustee to minimize future complications, not the least of which could potentially be plan disqualification and/or fiduciary impropriety.

- *Satisfactory repurchase obligation study:* Pre-transaction repurchase obligation studies are not usually necessary in first-stage transactions. Nonetheless, it is advisable for the lender to encourage the company to begin thinking about and planning for the repurchase obligation.

Overcoming Common Underwriting Obstacles

The nonproductive debt, the negative tangible net worth, the complexity of ESOP financing as it interrelates with so many other disciplines, the fiduciary risk, and the typical desire by sellers to limit their personal pledge of Section 1042 assets all serve to heighten the complexity of ESOP financing. A financing transaction that on one hand could be looked at like any other credit request becomes fairly complex when an ESOP is involved. Knowledge of how to creatively overcome the underwriting obstacles, as described below, can help sellers, companies, and service providers in choosing the best lender for their particular transaction and can help lenders successfully underwrite these transactions.

What Is an ESOP? Educating the Lender

Lenders need to be educated on the peculiarities of an ESOP transaction, including the accounting treatment, the difference between the inside and outside loan, fiduciary issues, benefit administration, and allocation issues. A lender needs to understand that benefit restrictions can limit the amount a company can "expense" in a given year. Loans need to be thoughtfully and prudently structured around such limitations. The ESOP could, for example, impair a company's ability to meet a standard cash flow recapture provision.

Although it is advisable to work with an experienced ESOP lender whenever possible, working with an existing financial institution may provide a company greater comfort, debt capacity, and financial flexibility. This is due to such an institution's competitive advantage in understanding a particular company's business. Introduce your lender to experienced financial advisors, attorneys, and plan administrators early in the feasibility process to give the lender sufficient time to learn and understand the nuances of the ESOP transaction.

Historical Financial Information

Often, an ESOP prospect has not previously borrowed much beyond a typical working capital line of credit with its local lender. Typically, the company has not been required to provide audited financials. The quality of reported earnings has never been questioned. The company has typically never been subject to the extensive due diligence on the historical financials that will be part of leveraged ESOP underwriting. Companies may resist, finding the process overwhelming and intrusive.

Overcoming this problem: The purpose of the lender's due diligence is to gain comfort with the company's historical ability to generate cash flow and use that as a benchmark to predict the company's future ability to do so. It is critical to the lender that the company assist in this process. It is an opportunity for the company to begin to partner with the lender. The better the lender understands the historical financial information and the company's revenue and margin sensitivities, the more confident the lender will be in calculating senior debt capacity for the borrower. Greater senior debt capacity has several advantages to the seller and company, such as favorable pricing, less of a pledge of Section 1042 assets in Section 1042 deals, less need for mezzanine and equity investors, and avoiding the complexities of multi-investor transactions.

Alternatives for evaluating historical numbers: In some instances, the lender will require an independent auditor to audit historical numbers. This is costly in both money and time. Alternatives include: (1) an audit of only the income statement, (2) third-party due diligence, and (3) the bank sending out its own field auditors to examine the books and records of the company.

Out of Size, Out of Market

A company should always strive to be in an important relationship to its primary financial institution. This means being the right size for its lender. It is not advisable to be either the smallest or largest client relationship for a lender. Therefore, smaller transactions are often best served with local banks. Unfortunately, the technical sophistication required for ESOP lending is often not found in these smaller financial institutions, and the larger financial institutions are not interested in traveling to remote locations for smaller-sized transactions.

Overcoming this problem: If the hurdle to educating the lender is too large, or the proposed ESOP transaction causes a company to "outgrow" its existing financial institution, a new lender may be necessary. To source an experienced lender, a company should talk with local attorneys, financial advisors, and plan administrators who have worked on ESOP transactions, call local companies that have ESOPs in place, and use the resources of organizations such as the NCEO and the ESOP Association for leads.

Lack of Creativity

ESOPs can be nonproductive debt. Lenders need to think creatively and understand how the ESOP fits into the whole context of corporate and shareholder objectives. Because these objectives can vary so much, each ESOP tends to have a unique structure.

Overcoming lack of creativity: For straightforward transactions in a more generic industry that do not burden the company's debt capacity, financing may be available from local or existing lenders. For more creative structures, a company will need to be more aggressive in its search process. The NCEO and the ESOP Association are excellent resources for names of companies and/or professionals who have participated in recent or similar ESOP transactions. In highly complex transactions, engaging a financial advisor to assist in deal structure, lender education, and debt placement can also prove beneficial.

What Is an ESOP? Educating Your Controller/CFO

The complexities of putting a leveraged ESOP in place often exceed the experience of the company's controller or chief financial officer. The lender will require significant forecasting and sensitivity analysis. The CFO will likely be responsible for negotiating the terms and conditions of the loan agreement without the requisite experience. However, the company typically does not have a long-term need for a CFO with higher credentials.

Overcoming this problem: Working with an experienced lender and an experienced financial advisor can mitigate this problem. Another solution is to formally engage a financial advisor to the transaction. This could be the company's accountant, an investment banker, an independent financial consultant, or a valuation professional. Financial advisors representing the company prepare the detailed forecasts and financial analysis that lenders require. To the extent the lender better understands the financial sensitivities of the company, the company may be able to negotiate more competitive credit arrangements. A company might also consider introducing its chief financial officer to CFOs from other ESOP companies to exchange ideas and information. Names of companies and candidates who may be interested in such networking are available through the NCEO and the ESOP Association.

What Is an ESOP? Educating the Lender's Loan Committee or Risk Approvers

Even when the loan officer understands ESOPs and ESOP lending, it won't help the company unless the financing institution's loan committee is also familiar with the particularities that make ESOP transactions look different from the typical deal they see. It is not unusual for an ESOP deal to get turned down or restructured in the loan committee process.

Overcoming this problem: Due diligence is not a one-way process solely involving the lending institution evaluating the company. Companies should also be evaluating the lending institution. ESOP loans are term loans. The lender will be an important business partner for at least several years. Companies are well advised to seek out the lending institution they feel would be the best business partner for the foreseeable future. Some "due diligence" questions companies might consider asking lenders include:

1. What is the financial institution's stability? This is *very* important. A decline in a lending institution's financial performance is often followed by a change in lending strategy and tightening of underwriting guidelines. A highly leveraged loan that was acceptable when the transaction closed may be considered too risky under a new analysis structure, particularly if the company's financial performance deviates from forecasts.

2. Has the lending institution recently been acquired, or is it a potential acquisition target? Mergers and acquisitions bring changes in management and can bring a change in loan underwriting guidelines.

3. Are there any management or strategic changes anticipated at the lending institution that would affect its credit policy?

4. Who will be the company's relationship manager going forward? Relationship managers (RMs) are the primary advocates for the company at the lending institution. RMs promote the company inside the bank. The company benefits from a long-term relationship with an RM who understands both ESOPs and the particular business.

5. How long has the lender been active in the company's market niche (size of company, size of transaction, ESOPs, industry, geographical location, deal structure, etc.)?

6. What is the likelihood of continued service by that lender to that market niche?

7. Has the company met senior management at the lending institution?

8. Does the company know how the loan approval process works? "Surprises" can be avoided by thorough due diligence on the prospective lending institution by the company.

Insufficient Collateral

It is in both the company's and lender's best interest to first provide for all credit required for ongoing operations, both revolver and term ("normal debt"). The loan value of corporate assets often does not cover both normal debt requirements *and* the proposed ESOP loan. Lenders need to be creative in structuring the transaction to best meet the seller's objectives without compromising the financial stability of the company. Table 7-2 above, which is repeated below, depicts this situation.

Table 7-2 (repeated). Example of an ESOP Term Loan Creating a Collateral Shortfall

Asset	Gross value	Advance rate	Loan value
Accounts receivable	$10,000,000	80%	$8,000,000
Inventory	$5,000,000	50%	2,500,000
Real estate	$5,000,000	70%	3,500,000
Fixed assets	$8,000,000	50%	4,000,000
Total loan value of collateral			$18,000,000
Less: existing revolver and term debt requirements			(10,000,000)
Collateral available for ESOP term loan			$8,000,000
Less: ESOP term loan			(20,000,000)
Collateral shortfall			$(12,000,000)

Overcoming this problem: In the example above, the financing question is how to structure the $12 million collateral shortfall. Creative structuring can often overcome a shortfall in the loan value of corporate assets. Ideas that have been successfully implemented include:

• *Having management investment in the transaction:* Management can invest directly, guarantee, or provide some sort of credit enhancement to bridge a financing gap. A benefit of this strategy is that it offsets the ESOP's inability to motivate key management employees. As a nondiscriminatory plan, the ESOP allocates to participants pro rata based on payroll, with a cap for highly compensated employees. This precludes key management from accumulating a disproportionate ownership stake. The downside of this strategy is that key managers often do not have significant outside net worth to provide a meaningful initial equity investment in the company.

- *Conversion of existing plan assets into employer securities:* Sometimes companies have been matching a 401(k) plan or providing attractive pension or profit-sharing benefits to their employees for a number of years. Where significant plan balances have accumulated, particularly when the assets in the plan have accumulated as a result of employer contributions, it is possible to reinvest a small portion of the balances from existing plan investments into employer securities, i.e., the ESOP. In the example above with the $12 million collateral shortfall, if the company had $40 million in 401(k) balances and $10 million of the $40 million were a result of the company match, it would not be unreasonable to consider the conversion of existing plan assets for a $5 million investment in the transaction. Though this does not completely fill the $12 million requirement, lenders are comforted by the employees' conviction in their company. Perhaps the lender could then feel comfortable holding an unsecured position for the remaining $7 million. Table 7-10 depicts how the transaction works. Note: Conversion of existing plan assets into employer securities entails careful consideration of a number of important ERISA as well as possible securities law issues and benefit issues. Companies must consult with experienced benefits counsel to verify the applicability of conversion to their particular plans. Very rarely can more than a small percentage of plan assets be safely transferred.

Table 7-10. Funding Example Using Conversion of Plan Assets	
Source of funds for seller	**Amount**
Secured by corporate assets	$8,000,000
"Undersecured" senior debt	7,000,000
Total senior ESOP financing	$15,000,000
Conversion of existing plan assets	5,000,000
Total funds to seller	$20,000,000

- *Use of seller notes:* The seller could choose to take proceeds from the ESOP in the form of a seller note (table 7-11). For example, using the $20 million ESOP loan request above, the seller could take a note for $6 million and perhaps negotiate with the lender to provide the additional $6 million on an undersecured basis. Benefits of seller notes include attractive interest rates to the seller (they are typically subordinated to bank debt and thereby earn a market rate of about 14%) and avoidance of a mezzanine and/or outside equity investor in the transaction. There are creative investment strategies the seller can use to enjoy the tax deferral of the Section 1042 benefit on all the sales proceeds, including subordinated notes.

Table 7-11. Funding Example Using Seller Notes	
Source of funds for seller	**Amount**
Secured by corporate assets	$8,000,000
"Undersecured" senior debt	6,000,000
Total senior ESOP financing	$14,000,000
Subordinated seller note	6,000,000
Total funds to seller	$20,000,000

- *Pledging of 1042 assets as collateral:* Issues and opportunities related to the pledge of 1042 assets as collateral are detailed above under "Section 1042 Benefit."

- *Mezzanine and equity financing:* A third party could provide subordinated debt or equity to bridge the gap between senior financing available and total financing requirements for a particular transaction. Financial advisors are helpful in sourcing mezzanine and equity investors whose investment strategy would fit with the particular company and in resolving the related equity allocation issues associated. This details of this type of financing are beyond the scope of this chapter.

- *Cash flow financing:* Some lenders will "underwrite" a company's cash flow, essentially providing debt in excess of the loan value of assets. A cash flow lender, in the above example, would provide the entire $20 million loan request if the credit met the particular lender's underwriting standards for such loans. General guidelines for "eligibility" for cash flow lending include:

— Stable historical revenues and margins (preferably in a non-cyclical industry).

— Minimum of three to five years in business.

— Revenues in excess of $50 million.

— EBITDAE in excess of $5 million.

— A senior debt to EBITDAE ratio of less than 3x. (This particular ratio changes from time to time with the expansion and contraction of the credit markets. It is also subject to change within particular lending institutions.)

— The loan should be amortized down to at or below the loan value of the borrower's assets by the end of the fourth year.

- *Second lien/junior secured:* To fill a gap between the senior credit rates and mezzanine rates, a new product is emerging called second lien or junior secured debt. These are lenders who will lend against the existing collateral pool at a rate approximately halfway between senior rates and mezzanine rates.

- *Lease financing:* Leasing companies will often advance a higher advance rate against fixed assets than traditional lenders. Another reason to look into lease financing is that there may be an opportunity to do off-balance-sheet financing at a lower cost. For example, S corporations do not need depreciation expense. Therefore, if they pass the depreciation off to someone else in exchange for a lower financing cost, they might be better off.

- *Government credit enhancement:* State and local governments are increasingly seeing ESOPs as an effective transition vehicle to keep local jobs and tax revenue. Many states have provided credit enhancements to the senior lenders to entice them to lend more to an ESOP situation. Check with your local government's economic development office.

- *High-yield debt:* Depending on market conditions, ESOP companies have successfully accessed the public marketplace as a source of cash for the transaction.

Inability to Provide Cash Flow Financing

One solution to insufficient collateral is to structure the loan as a "cash flow" loan. The total credit facilities exceed the loan value of the collateral by some multiple of cash flow, depending on the strength of the credit. Some financial institutions are not interested in the credit risk associated with cash flow lending, regardless of how well structured.

Overcoming this problem: The simplest solution is to seek out a lending institution that has a "leveraged finance" division familiar with cash flow lending. Basically, leveraged finance lenders consider a company's primary asset to be that company's ability to predictably generate cash flow. This differs from an "asset-based" approach, which evaluates debt capacity based on the loan value of unencumbered corporate assets. Covenants monitor EBITDAE (earnings before interest, taxes, depreciation, amortization, and employee benefit expense related to the ESOP) versus tangible net worth. Unfortunately, many ESOP transactions are too small to fit the target profile of the leveraged finance units of major money center banks. Nonetheless, a company can often successfully negotiate (depending on market conditions) 12 to 24 months' cash flow "overadvance" from lenders who perhaps are not technically "leveraged finance" or "cash flow" lenders. The ability to do this was assumed in both the "seller note" and "conversion of plan assets" examples above. Companies need a solid financial plan, sensitizing revenues, and earnings to get the lender comfortable in taking on the cash flow risk.

Chapter 8

Mature ESOP Considerations

Mary Josephs and Neal Hawkins

Experience is always an excellent teacher. A treasure trove of lessons has emerged from both hugely successful and less successful ESOP companies who implemented Esops in the 1970s, 1980s, and 1990s. First, let us define a "mature ESOP" as one that has substantially repaid seller financing, one that has been in place more than seven years, and/ or one whose company has experienced significantly different performance outcomes from transaction projections over time.

As a child, one of the authors was repeatedly told about "the five P's": Prior Planning Prevents Poor Performance. How begrudgingly we heard these words as schoolchildren! As with much wisdom, it takes an adult lens to appreciate it. In the case of ESOPs, it is helpful to plan the design of new ESOPs, the restructuring of existing ESOPs, and the examination of issues such as ESOP feasibility and sustainability by looking through the lens of experience and taking advantage of lessons learned.[1] Examples include:

• Planning for repurchase of the equity from the ESOP participants as the ESOP plan and workers age.

• Comprehensive analysis during the original plan design with consideration for targeted benefit levels, overall equity allocation, and future claims on capital.

• Proactive and dynamic planning for plan allocations and distributions, including sensitivity analyses.

---

1. See the lessons collected in the book *Don't Do That: Common Mistakes in Operating an ESOP and What to Do About Them* (Oakland, CA: NCEO, 2010).

- Long-term capital planning, assessing the company's ability to meet corporate and strategic objectives, including maximizing shareholder value (e.g., growth capital and capital for shareholder liquidity)

Capital

The types of capital available to a mature or maturing ESOP will differ based upon the company's size, balance sheet, historical performance, growth opportunities, overall industry dynamics, capital markets dynamics, and capital structure. Leadership plays a critical role as well. Although it is sometimes overlooked, ESOP restructuring could be an alternative for accessing capital needed to continue to drive growth in shareholder value.

Why is capital needed for mature ESOPs? A common reason for raising capital is to refinance other parts of the capital structure such as retiring mezzanine debt, seller notes, and/or warrants. A best practice of any efficient company is to minimize its cost of debt by refinancing out more expensive debt with lower-cost capital.

Management incentives may also require a company to raise capital. Many ESOP companies incentivize key managers to drive value for all participants, and when the company is successful, those incentives need to be paid out as managers retire or leave. Depending on the timing of these payouts, some mature ESOPs do not have the cash readily available, therefore creating a need for third-party financing.

Like any company, mature ESOP companies need capital to finance growth plans and/or acquisitions. Due to the unique ownership structure of an ESOP with employees as owners, the shareholder base does not have the financial wherewithal to invest equity to grow the business. Instead, the growth of an ESOP company has to be financed with debt.

Just as they may need financing to pay out management incentives, some mature ESOP companies also find the need to finance the repurchase obligation. For example, when a key long-term employee retires who has accumulated a sizable portion of ownership, it may require the company to raise capital to fund that obligation.

In addition to external sources of capital, a unique internal capital source can actually come from refinancing the existing ESOP loan. The refinance allows capital to be freed up as the internal loan is stretched out. Shares are allocated less quickly, and the increase in the repurchase obligation slows. Please note, however, that this is a highly complicated process and should only be analyzed with experienced professionals. Fiduciary integrity must be the guide. There must be a valid business reason to pursue a loan stretch-out.

Revising the Distribution Policy

Revising the ESOP's distribution policy can allow the company to preserve company cash with longer distributions. By not having to pay out in a lump sum, the company can moderate repayments, lessening the current burden on cash flow. This can be particularly helpful with large distributions. Sometimes companies have a more delayed distribution schedule for account balances over a specified threshold.

There are some considerations that should be taken into account when extending the distribution policy. One major drawback is that it enables participants to remain invested in stock. This may or may not be deemed favorable to a particular company. Interestingly, before the financial crisis of 2008, there was a bias that it was a bad thing to have employees remain in company stock. This may still be a company's perspective. Thinking through long-term capital and capital flexibility needs will help guide the company to the appropriate use of cash and debt capacity.

Partial to Full ESOP and S Corporation Conversion

The exemption from federal (and usually state) income tax on corporate earnings following the conversion to a 100% ESOP-owned S corporation will provide additional cash flow. This incremental cash flow can be reinvested for growth or used to fund the repurchase obligation. In addition, during the conversion there is the ability to design (or redesign) the ESOP benefit over a longer period of time.

Patient Capital and Examples

ESOPs are no different from privately held businesses with the need for patient capital to support long-term transitions. Although this may seem somewhat counterintuitive, the ESOP itself is amongst the most patient sources of capital. Bank facilities can mature in three to seven years. Private equity generally looks for four- to seven-year exits. Esops, on the other hand, turn over with the life cycle of their employee-participants. Esops, while not perhaps as patient as a family business owner (although this is debatable), are an outstanding form of patient capital.

There are five major types of patient capital, most of which are covered within this book:

- The ESOP itself
- Private placements (discussed in chapter 9)
- Equity (discussed in chapter 9)
- IPOs
- Seller financing (discussed in chapter 11)

Strategic, long-term capital planning is crucial for ESOP companies. Understanding future capital requirements and the preparation of dynamic strategies to accommodate the company's needs over time will support long-term sustainability and growth in share value.

Sale or Termination

Sale of an ESOP Company

In considering the sale of an ESOP company, the question should not be "Should or should we not remain ESOP-owned?" but rather "What is the best strategy to drive shareholder value and optimize the company's objectives?" We believe it is difficult to surpass the value proposition of employee ownership, which has been demonstrated by research on the topic. However, sometimes selling the company or terminating the plan is the superior alternative. In such cases, this is not negative but rather the right thing to do at the right time.

One reason to sell an ESOP company is an unsolicited offer that is too good to pass up.[2] Similarly, a sale might also occur when a strategic

---

2. See *Responding to Acquisition Offers in ESOP Companies* (Oakland, CA: NCEO, 2011).

buyer is willing to pay a premium for synergies and/or the prospect of acquiring access to a new market or product. The onus is on the board of directors to determine whether the sale is in the best interest of all shareholders.

In other cases the sale of a company is driven by the lack of succession leadership.[3] Some successful companies fail to focus on developing successors for the key individuals within an organization; they then decide the only way to continue to grow shareholder value is to sell to a strategic or financial buyer with the professional experience to grow the firm going forward. In other situations, a sale might be out of the ESOP's control, with a majority non-ESOP shareholder pushing a transaction.

Finally, the sale of the business might be needed to fund the repurchase obligation. Although the repurchase obligation is traditionally funded with either cash flow from the business or debt capacity, there are situations where those capital alternatives fall short. When future cash flows are constrained due to looming repurchase obligations and the company has no additional debt capacity, a sale may be the only viable alternative.

Terminating an ESOP

The most common reason for an ESOP plan to be terminated is that a non-ESOP shareholder wishes to regain 100% equity ownership. This type of plan termination usually occurs when the ESOP is a minority shareholder.

A termination of an ESOP can also be driven by management's view that the ESOP is not a valued benefit plan. Corporate culture and communication around the ESOP directly affect the success of the ESOP plan. In some situations, the ESOP benefits (such as greater worker productivity) which might have been the main reasons for adopting an ESOP do not materialize. The ESOP structure itself might also influence corporate culture negatively due to have- and have-not issues. When inequality of ownership happens, management might find itself having to explain why some employees have the added benefit while others do not. This can lead to management terminating the plan to alleviate the internal cultural tension.

---

3.   See *Leadership Development and Succession* (Oakland, CA: NCEO, 2012).

Any termination or sale transaction has to be financed with third-party debt and equity. The ESOP cannot take back a note.

Best Practices

Ending where we began, any best practice includes planning: In real estate the value mantra is "location, location, location." For ESOP companies, we suggest "planning, planning, planning." Long-term capital planning protects a company from unforeseen surprises that could limit long-term flexibility and options. This planning should include proactive information gathering, including market dynamics, industry dynamics, strategic planning, and how plan implementation affects benefit levels. This planning can develop a road map of objectives for a mature ESOP company.

Furthermore, explore and analyze different solutions under different sensitivities. Evaluate solutions both quantitatively and qualitatively against predetermined goals. Management needs to understand the short- and long-term impacts of all alternatives to make the most informed decision.

A best practice for any privately held company is to have independent board members or advisory board members to give the company new perspectives and challenge what might be entrenched thinking.

Finally, work with experienced professionals. Fiduciary oversight of existing ESOPs can never be taken lightly. The company should have a highly experienced team that is proficient with companies of its size, industry, and ESOP dynamics.

Chapter 9

Types of Capital

Neal Hawkins and John Solimine

This chapter focuses on the types of capital companies can think about in evaluating (1) sources of funds for an initial ESOP transaction; (2) sources of funds for mature ESOPs to support growth; (3) sources of funds to support second-stage transactions; (4) sources of funds to support management, individual shareholder, and/or repurchase obligations; (5) sources of funds to support growth initiatives; and (6) sources for other needs. One way to think about capital is to divide these sources into three broad categories: senior capital, junior capital, and equity. The type of capital best suited for a particular situation depends on many things, including company size, amount of capital needed, cash flow, collateral coverage, ownership objectives, equity allocation, and the use of the capital. As a borrower, the company needs to evaluate and carefully weigh many factors to obtain the optimal capital structure.

Senior Capital

Senior capital is one of the most diverse and commonly used sources of capital in an ESOP structure. The capital that senior lenders provide is usually the least risky, involves the least amount of invasive diligence, and is the lowest priced. A senior lender provides two main forms of loans to borrowers:

1. Revolving line of credit ("revolver")
2. Term loan.

A broad range of firms are classified as senior lenders, from large national institutions (i.e., Bank of America, JP Morgan Chase, Wells Fargo, Fifth Third Bank, etc.) to small community banks. It is important to recognize that non-bank financial institutions, such as Prudential

Capital and GE, are competing for senior credit market share. The type of lender or lenders a borrower will choose depends on many factors, including the size of the overall commitment, the type of loan (described below), the industry, and the need for flexibility.

Asset-Based Loans

An asset-based loan is a revolving line of credit and/or term loan that heavily relies on the assets of the borrower. Asset-based loans tie the size of the loan to the value of the company's assets. The most common assets that a lender will underwrite are accounts receivables; raw and finished inventory (collectively, generally supporting a revolving credit facility); and/or real estate, plants, and equipment (collectively, generally supporting a term facility). A lender will perform due diligence, including lender-approved appraisals and field exams, on each asset category. Sometimes this results in better advance rates, and sometimes it might result in additional eliminations or curtailment of certain assets due to the low probability of realizing cash from an asset (e.g., a receivable over 120 days old). Given the high dependence on assets, a lender will require the company to submit a borrowing base certificate either daily, weekly, or monthly. In addition, a field exam (similar to the initial field exam) of the assets would be performed either annually or semiannually. Depending on the asset coverage, a lender may require a sweep account that would reduce the revolver balance by the cash on hand at the end of each day. Finally, an asset-based lender will most likely require the borrower to utilize a "lockbox" feature to allow the lender to apply all incoming cash to reduce the revolver. The company then reborrows for working capital as needed.

Even though the lender focuses on the assets of the borrower as a primary source of repayment, the lender still underwrites the cash flow of the business. A successful operation is always the preferred repayment strategy. Asset-based lending is most commonly used when borrowers (1) are asset-rich, and a lender can underwrite the value of the assets after applying certain advance rates; (2) are in cyclical industries; (3) have unstable cash flow; (4) are small and have little to no repayment history; (5) are highly leveraged; or (6) have large working capital needs. Table 9-1 provides an example of a borrowing base and the borrowing capacity calculation.

Table 9-1. Example Borrowing Base			
Asset	Dollar amount	Advance rate	Availability
Accounts receivables (under 90 days)	$10,000,000	85%	$8,500,000
Inventory (raw and finished)	$8,000,000	50%	4,000,000
			$12,500,000
Less: current loan outstanding			7,000,000
Loan availability			$5,500,000

Benefits: Asset-based lending is generally competitively priced and, for asset-rich companies, can provide the greatest amount of senior credit (as compared to cash flow).

Considerations: Some feel the administrative requirements of regular borrowing base certificates, lockboxes, and regular field exams are cumbersome. Furthermore, this type of credit is not competitive for service-based or other asset-light businesses.

Cash Flow Loan

A cash flow loan, as its name implies, is a loan that is based on the future cash flow of the borrower. A cash flow lender will require a borrower to provide consistent and stable earnings over a length of time (usually at least three to five historical years). More consistency in year-over-year cash flows allows a lender to gain comfort in the ability of the borrower to achieve future projected cash flows. The lender also underwrites industry, competitive, geographical, political, etc., dynamics to understand key trends that might negatively affect the borrower's cash flow. While the lender is primarily looking at the cash flow of the borrower to repay the loan, the lender will also generally require a first lien on all assets as a secondary source of repayment.

Cash flow loans are flexible and can be structured in various forms. The most common structure is the use of a revolver and term loan. The revolver provides the borrower with the capital to fund its working capital needs, while the term loan provides capital for long-term investments (such as the initial ESOP purchase, repurchasing stock, funding acquisitions, and meeting growth needs with expanded equipment, etc.). Term loans have an amortization schedule determined by general lending market conditions and by the flexibility needed by the borrower in certain years. A key underwriting consideration for cash-flow lending is an analysis of the cash inflow of the business compared to the fixed charges over a set period (also referred to as the fixed charge coverage ratio). The stronger this ratio, the better able the company is to cover its fixed charges. Therefore, the stronger this ratio, the better the terms and pricing the borrower can expect. With any ESOP transaction, the borrower should confirm that the post-closing tax savings are factored into the lender's free cash flow analysis. On the other hand, cash outflow from the repurchase obligation should also be factored into the fixed charge calculation.

In most stable markets, lenders of traditional cash flow term loans will provide a term loan with a five-year tenure and amortizations (depending on market dynamics and unique company circumstances) of between five and ten years. The revolving credit facility may either have the same tenure as the corresponding term loan or may only be extended on a one-year basis. The pricing of a specific term loan and revolver will be based on market conditions and the overall risk profile of the company.

Benefits: Cash flow loans allow a borrower the lowest cost capital with a good deal of flexibility for stable middle-market companies that are in service or asset-light industries.

Considerations: Smaller businesses with mixed earnings history may not be able to access this type of loan without additional collateral such as a guarantee or pledge back of securities.

Term Loan B

A term loan B is an offshoot from a traditional term loan described above. The term loan B allows more flexibility on the required amortization (e.g., only 1% per annum). Term B loans generally offer a maturity date after the revolver and any other senior financing. This loan would still be provided by banking institutions but would have a second priority to the cash flow and assets of the borrower. As you might imagine, this is riskier from a senior lender's viewpoint and would be priced accordingly.

This type of term loan is usually provided to stable, larger middle-market cash flow clients (usually with greater than $15 million in EBITDA). Overall market lending conditions dictate the availability for this type of capital. Due to the subordinated senior position and lower amortization, the cost of capital is higher on a term loan B than a traditional term loan.

Multi-Bank Financing

When the size of the senior credit request exceeds the preferred hold position for one bank, the borrower will benefit from having multiple banks provide capital. Raising this capital can be done through multiple channels; the most common arrangement in the middle market is a "club deal." In a club deal, there are usually two to three lenders who provide capital to a borrower under the same loan agreement. Depending on the borrower's financing relationship, the group of lenders can be arranged by the CFO, by a lead bank, or by an investment banker helping the company arrange the financing. For even larger credit requests, a borrower can engage an investment bank or advisor to help arrange and syndicate the senior financing. Sometimes the borrower will choose one bank to act as the lead bank and/or use an advisor (investment bank) or relationships to fill in the club deal.

Another approach is to pay for a single bank to take the risk to fill in remaining participant lenders. This process can either be done on a "best efforts" or "fully underwritten" basis. The former is done with the lead bank raising the capital on behalf of the borrower with the lender's best efforts (no legal commitment) to secure the total capital requested. In a fully underwritten syndication, the lead bank will commit to the entire capital request and then raise capital from the other banks.

Benefits of a Club Deal: For companies that have an advisor who knows natural team players to fill out their capital needs and/or themselves have significant relationships with capital partners who are likely participants in the proposed facilities, club deals ensure control of the partners, generally have the lowest all-in fees, and generally form a path to a smooth closing.

Considerations of Club Deal: Sometimes companies do not have existing relationships with optimal financial service providers to fill out a lending team that best fits their needs.

Benefits of an Investment Bank "Best Efforts" Deal: For borrowers who have high confidence that the particular credit facilities will clear market, and who have general knowledge as to who the eventual bank group might be, this is a cost-effective strategy to align all the right interests for the borrower.

Considerations for an Investment Bank "Best Efforts" Deal: The lead bank has no obligation to source all the required capital for the prescribed transaction. If timing and dollars at close are deal-critical issues, a "best efforts" deal might not be optimal.

Benefits of an Investment Bank "Underwritten" Deal: A firm underwriting is just that. This assures the borrower that the lender is taking the full risk to secure the ascribed financing to support the underlying transaction.

Considerations for an Investment Bank "Underwritten" Deal: With certainty comes risk from the underwriter's point of view. This will incur the highest up-front fees.

Overall Observations: New trends in banking suggest an ever-increasing focus on the total relationship. This means that the company should give serious consideration to how many bank(s) it can truly keep happy. Traditional commercial banks need more than interest income to really support a profitable win-win relationship. The company should be strategic and should not spread itself too thick or too thin.

Any multi-bank financing will have higher costs and fees than that of a single-bank financing. Each lender will have return hurdles based upon the risk of the loan and other services available. This analysis will drive the pricing and the fees for the entire loan facility. An ESOP borrower must select a lead bank that understands not only the syndications market but also ESOPs as well as the company's industry and geography. Also, as the lead bank, it must have the ability and influence to educate other lenders on the unique characteristics of the company's credit facilities.

Private Placement

Capital markets for the middle market exist beyond traditional commercial banks and non-bank financial institutions. These private lenders, most commonly for ESOPs, are insurance companies, but can also include mutual funds, pension funds, and hedge funds. The benefits of using a private placement are the flexibility in the form of loan tenure and amortization schedule that is offered to the borrower. The usual terms for a private placement will include a tenure of six to ten years and a fixed interest rate for the borrower. In low interest rate environments, it might make sense for a borrower to use a debt instrument that allows the rate to be fixed for the duration of the loan.

A private placement is not for all borrowers because the investor usually requires a size threshold (greater than $15 million in EBITDA). Another consideration for the borrower is that the cost of financing can be higher for the tenure flexibility. In most loans, the investor will also require a prepayment penalty for a period of time (usually for the first two to three years on a declining scale). Finally, the investor may also request that the borrower obtain a "shadow" rating from a rating agency to assess the risk of the borrower. The rating is provided only to the private placement lenders and is not publicly disclosed, and it usually is defined as an NAIC rating.

Benefits: For certain companies (those rated NAIC 2), private placements can offer a superior, low-cost, and highly flexible capital alternative.

Considerations: Few ESOP companies are rated. The resulting "fixed cost" financing is higher-priced than the current floating rate. The company should in each situation analyze long-term objectives and ascertain whether a private placement could enhance shareholder value.

Real Estate

A borrower can obtain a loan against any real estate that is currently owned by the corporation. A lender will underwrite a term loan for real estate similar to that of a traditional home mortgage by obtaining an appraisal for the land and any buildings from a third party. A common requirement from the lender is an environmental study to test whether there are contaminants in the soil. If any contaminants are found, it could limit the amount lent against the assets or entirely restrict the use of the assets. The typical advance rate against the market value of real estate can range from zero to 70% depending on location, size, and use of the asset. The loan against the real estate usually has a longer amortization than a traditional term loan and is based upon market conditions (usually 10 to 20 years). The real estate loan will have a tenure and pricing that mirrors a term loan. Recently, as evidenced by private equity strategies, considering the sale and leaseback of company real estate has been part of an overall capital management strategic analysis.

Junior Capital

Unitranche Debt

Unitranche debt is a newer type of financial instrument and combines elements of various tranches of debt, most commonly a blend of senior and junior debt. This instrument allows for the simplification and expedition of the lending process. Unitranche lenders provide more flexibility to small business owners in the form of more true cash flow lending. With a unitranche credit facility, a borrower will have one lender and will be subject to only one interest rate. The interest rate is generally a blend of current prevailing rates for senior debt and subordinated notes. For example, if senior lenders are offering an interest rate of 5% and mezzanine providers are offering an interest rate of 15%, the blended interest rate on unitranche would be around 10%. This type of debt instrument is typically used in leveraged buyout and acquisition processes. An increasing number of lenders, usually non-bank financial institutions, offer this product. The availability of this type of debt will be dependent on market conditions. Unitranche lenders usually require a borrower to have a minimum EBITDA of $5–$10 million.

Benefits: Unitranche financing allows a middle-market borrower the ease of accessing both senior and junior capital from one lender.

Considerations: The unitranche lender will still require the same level of due diligence as any other junior capital provider. Depending on the objectives of the borrower, unitranche financing may not provide the lowest cost of capital.

Junior Capital

Junior capital is a form of debt that is subordinate to senior lenders but still a debt obligation. In the capital structure, a junior lender is lower in priority of repayment than other forms of senior debt discussed above. Often, junior debt is an unsecured form of debt, meaning there are no assets or collateral pledged against the loan. This type of debt is often used in conjunction with senior debt, usually after senior financing has been maximized. This capital is provided by various lenders, which include institutional and mezzanine lenders or even a seller in a transaction. For the increased risk, junior capital providers demand a higher return or interest rate than senior lenders. Other forms of junior debt can be debentures and second mortgages. The pricing or returns for a junior lender vary by company but usually include one or more of the following: cash interest, paid-in-kind (PIK) interest, and/or synthetic equity. The returns required by junior capital vary with market conditions, transaction risk, and borrower size, but usually range from 12% to 18%. A borrower with $10–$25 million in EBITDA usually can access this market.

Junior capital is commonly found in transactions as gap financing between the senior lenders and the equity holders. In ESOP transactions, subordinated debt financing is most commonly used to maximize the cash received at close by the selling shareholders. Other alternatives to junior capital are discussed below, but junior capital is a viable debt solution in some transactions. In any transaction, a senior lender must agree upon the terms and conditions of any junior or mezzanine financing. Beyond agreeing on the terms, a senior lender will also require an agreement (usually referred to as an inter-creditor agreement) that explains the rights the senior lender has over any junior capital. One common example is when a senior lender requires any cash interest payments to stop and be converted into paid-in-kind interest in the event of a default. Finally, the senior lender will also require that any junior capital have a longer maturity than the senior debt.

Benefits: A junior lender allows a borrower to access additional capital beyond the senior debt market. In an ESOP buyout, a third-party junior lender may help provide additional cash at close for selling shareholders.

Considerations: A junior lender will perform a higher level of financial due diligence than would be required by a senior lender subsequently taking longer to close. A borrower will also have to balance the needs of a senior lender against those of the junior lender.

Mezzanine Financing

Mezzanine financing refers to a source of capital that usually combines characteristics of both debt and equity. Similar to junior capital, mezzanine capital is used to supplement bank debt and equity as a source of capital. As described above, mezzanine lenders are subordinated to any outstanding senior debt. Mezzanine financing can be structured in various ways; a common structure involves the borrower receiving a portion of the principal in interest (both cash and PIK) and receiving the remainder in the form of an equity stake. The term for mezzanine financing is six to ten years, with returns typically in the 15%–22% range based upon the market conditions and risk of the investment. A borrower with significant cash flow, historically high performance, and positive recognition within its industry can access this market. Borrowers look to mezzanine financing when they are unable to secure other forms of capital for various reasons (e.g., lack of collateral), or to provide more capital in a transaction. Sources for mezzanine investors include pension funds, private investors, mutual funds, insurance companies, and banks.

There are many similarities between junior lenders and mezzanine lenders when used in ESOP transactions, and the source of capital will depend on the risk of the transaction. In general, mezzanine financing is usually more accessible to the average middle-market borrower, while junior capital is used for larger middle-market transactions. Like junior capital, mezzanine financing is subject to the same terms and conditions as a subordinated lender (see above for the usual subordination terms).

Benefits: Mezzanine financing is another source of capital to middle-market borrowers that might decrease the overall cost of capital for a company. Mezzanine financing may also be a good source of capital for borrowers in industries that are not able to access senior credit markets.

Considerations: Mezzanine lenders may carry a higher cost of debt than other alternatives due to the equity repurchase at the investment's end. A mezzanine lender may also require certain board rights and/or seats, depending on the risk of the borrower.

Equity

Common Stock

Common stock represents the most basic form of ownership in a company and usually conveys voting rights. Common stockholders, as owners, participate in the performance of the company. The value of common stock can move up and down based on company performance and the market's perceptions of the company. This form of equity allows the holder to share in the company's profits through dividend payments, although dividends are not guaranteed, or through the equity growth. A common stock holder is subordinate to all outstanding debt obligations in the event of a liquidation (this includes senior debt, bonds, junior capital, preferred stock, and all other debt holders). This makes common stockholders residual owners in that they have a claim on the assets that remain after all other parties have been repaid. Common stock is the riskiest form of investment for an investor and also affords the holder unlimited upside.

How a company is structured from an ownership perspective dictates the types of common stock that can be issued to shareholders. For example, a C corporation can have different classes of stock, while an S corporation can only have one class of stock. Any ESOP transaction must be structured to take into account the pre- and post-ownership tax status of the company. An ESOP sponsor planning to become a 100% ESOP-owned S corporation (with its attendant tax advantages) should avoid selling or issuing stock outside the ESOP. So how do ESOP companies attract financing that might require some form of equity (i.e., junior capital or mezzanine capital) and still be 100% owned by the ESOP? The answer is through synthetic equity instruments that are not classified as common stock but provide the same economic value as equity.

Benefits: Common equity is the most stable form of capital for a company. The common equity holders have the ability to participate in the profits and equity gains of a company going forward. The common equity holders have the ability to elect the board of directors that governs the company.

Considerations: Common equity holders have the most risk at stake, given that their investment or repayment is not guaranteed. Common equity holders are usually the last in line during a liquidation of the assets.

Synthetic Equity

Synthetic equity has the same rewards and risks of owning stock without having a direct investment in that stock. This form of equity simulates or mirrors the returns of owning stock and benefits from increases in stock value. Stated differently, synthetic equity dilutes any common stock holders. Synthetic equity can be a way for owners and management to give employees an incentive tied to the equity growth of the company. This instrument allows synthetic equity holders exposure to the upside of the company performance without owning true shares of the company. Examples of synthetic equity include stock-equivalent units, or "phantom stock," which mirror stock ownership; equity-based deferred compensation plans; and stock appreciation rights, or "SARs," which mirror the economics of an option by only allowing the holder the right to share in an increase in the company's stock value. Synthetic equity can be issued for performance or can also be used in conjunction with a debt instrument to enhance the yield. Other contractual rights to acquire equity of the company, such as options and warrants, are also referred to as synthetic equity.

Within ESOP transactions, synthetic equity is usually an important part of any transaction. In situations where the management team has little to no ownership, SARs are commonly used to incentivize and compensate the management team. SARs align the interests of the management team and the ESOP to drive shareholder value, which in turn increases the value of the SARs. Another common use for synthetic equity is to enhance the return to subordinated lenders in 100%

ESOP S corporation transactions. These subordinated lenders can be outside institutional investors (i.e., those described above) and may also be selling shareholders who receive notes in exchange for selling their equity. Warrants as a form of synthetic equity can be a powerful tool in structuring subordinated debt to allow the borrower increased cash flow flexibility. Warrants may be a viable solution for the subordinated lender to supplement a portion of cash interest in the form of an equity upside. The reduction in cash interest may allow for a senior lender to provide more cost-effective financing for the transaction.

The S corporation ESOP anti-abuse rules under Section 409(p) of the Internal Revenue Code serve to limit the amount of synthetic equity that can be used. Borrowers should consult with their advisors to ensure compliance with these and other rules when using synthetic equity.

Benefits: Synthetic equity allows for investors who are not common stock holders the ability to participate in the growth of a company. For 100% S corporation ESOPs, synthetic equity allows non-ESOP shareholders or management the ability to continue to participate in the equity growth of a company.

Considerations: It is important to understand the dilution of existing common stock caused by the issuance of synthetic equity. Synthetic equity usually has a set time period that requires the equity to be repurchased or converted into a predetermined number of common stock shares.

Private Equity

Private equity consists of capital sourced primarily from institutional investors and funds that is invested directly into private companies or used to buy out public companies. This form of equity investment is not usually traded on a public stock exchange. A private equity investment usually is made by a private equity firm, a venture capital firm, or an angel investor. This form of equity is provided to a company to facilitate expansion, fund new technologies, make acquisitions, or restructure the company's operations or ownership. Private equity funds are usually limited partnerships with investors such as insurance companies, pension funds, endowments, banks, and high-net-worth individuals. These funds and their limited partners invest to receive equity-like returns, as measured in both internal rate of return and return on equity. Private equity is used for a limited period of time depending on the type of investment, the industry, and the exit strategy (usually between three and ten years, with an average life of five years). Liquidity strategies for private equity investments can include an initial public offering (IPO), strategic sale, sale to another private equity firm, management buy-out (MBO), or an ESOP. Some examples of private equity investment strategies include leveraged buyouts, venture capital, growth capital, mezzanine financing, and distressed investments.

The typical private equity investor likes to gain majority control of the investment as part of investing equity. The remaining equity will be retained by the selling shareholder with a separate potion being allocated to incentivize management. With privately held buyouts, the private equity firm might also structure a portion of the seller's consideration as an earnout—a payment made only if certain performance metrics are accomplished.

Most transactions are structured by the private equity firm to use the maximum amount of debt to minimize the investment by the private equity firm. The lower the initial investment by the private equity firm, the higher potential return over time. Table 9-2 provides an example of return on investment.

Private equity usually makes its profits in one of two ways, or a combination thereof. The first is to grow cash flow either through top-line revenue growth or a reduction in costs or increase in efficiencies that decrease costs. The second way an investment is profitable is through industry dynamics that allow the private equity firm to sell its investment for a higher multiple cash flow.

Benefits: Private equity investors can provide a viable solution for shareholders looking to realize a majority transition of their ownership in the form of cash. Private equity owners also bring a depth of knowledge on acquisitions, efficiencies in operations, and management expertise.

Considerations: Private equity has a limited investment period that will need to be monetized in the future, usually through a subsequent sale. Most private equity transactions involve a capital structure that maximizes leverage, which could hinder the growth of the company in a downturn. In some private equity buyouts a selling shareholder's consideration is paid in the contingent form of an earnout.

Table 9-2. Return on Assets: Private Equity Transaction

Capital structure	Highly leveraged transaction	Lower leveraged transaction
Senior financing	$10,000,000	$10,000,000
Subordinated financing	5,000,000	4,000,000
Equity	5,000,000	6,000,000
Total enterprise value	$20,000,000	$20,000,000
Value of equity in 5 years	$8,000,000	$8,000,000
Return on investment (calculated as increase in enterprise value / initial equity investment)	60%	33%

Chapter 10

Providers of Capital

Neal Hawkins and John Solimine

There are various ways by which a private company can raise capital without having to issue shares on a public market. These alternatives include senior lenders, junior capital providers, private equity, 401(k) capital, venture capital, and many others. Each alternative has its own advantages and disadvantages along with its own degree of risk.

Commercial Banks

Commercial banks are financial institutions and intermediaries that mainly focus on providing loans to established businesses, usually acting as a senior lender. A commercial bank can provide a wide variety of secured and unsecured financing, including term loans, revolving credit facilities, letters of credit, mortgage loans, and bond financing, among others, for various types of businesses and corporations. These financial institutions are federally insured by the FDIC and are governed by specific banking laws. Simply put, a bank's main purpose is to take deposits from individuals and businesses and lend those proceeds at a higher interest rate than it pays on the deposits. Nowadays, banks also provide a range of different products for customers, such as swaps, cash collections, wealth management, leasing, and investment banking services.

Commercial banks continue to be a prominent source for debt capital. As described elsewhere in this book, a company may obtain a cash flow-based loan with unsecured collateral and cash flow covenants. Also, a company may obtain an asset-based loan with secured collateral and working capital covenants. Usually these loans are monitored through loan covenants, collateral monitoring, and risk ratings. A commercial bank prices a loan based on a number of considerations, including the cost of funds, risk factors, market factors, and overall profitability. Commercial banks can be found in various sizes ranging from multinational banks to small community banks. A borrower should determine the needs of the company now and going forward when selecting a banking partner.

Non-Bank Financial Institutions

A non-bank financial institution is a financial institution that does not accept deposits like a traditional bank but still provides credit and other lending products similar to a bank. These institutions are not regulated by a national banking regulatory agency. Examples of this type of institution are insurance companies, pension funds, cashier's check issuers, currency exchanges, and pawn shops. A non-bank financial institution can offer services that banks do, such as loans, credit facilities, underwriting, money markets, and acquisition financing. Non-bank financial institutions raise their capital from insurance providers, high-net worth individuals, pension funds, endowments, hedge funds, and the public market.

The number of these institutions has increased significantly in recent years because retail, industrial, and venture capital companies have entered the lending business. Another driver for an increase in the number of non-bank financial institutions is investors who are searching for modest yield returns in a low interest rate environment. Other services that can be provided include investment, risk pooling, and market brokering.

Mezzanine Firms

Mezzanine capital is subordinated debt or preferred equity that is senior only to that of the common shares. This type of financing can be provided by many institutions, including commercial banks, private equity firms, specialty mezzanine firms, and hedge funds. Mezzanine financing can be structured either as debt, typically a subordinated note or unsecured loan, or through preferred stock. Due to the subordination of this financing, this type of capital is priced more aggressively than a senior loan. Mezzanine capital providers usually seek "all-in" returns in the range of 15% to 25% due to this increased risk. Also, these lenders seek their returns from three main sources: cash interest payments, payment-in-kind (PIK) interest, and equity ownership through a warrant or preferred stock purchase. Mezzanine capital is an attractive source of capital for companies looking to finance a growth strategy, acquisition, or buyout without giving up majority control. Depending on the type of investment a mezzanine provider may require a board seat as a voting member or as an advisory member. A borrower should understand the complete loan and investment the mezzanine lender is making in its company.

Private Equity

A private equity investment is one consisting of an equity investment in companies that are not publicly traded. These investments are made by private equity firms, venture capital firms, or angel investors. The most common private equity investment strategies include leveraged buyouts, growth capital, venture capital, mezzanine capital, and distressed investments. The majority of private equity consists of institutional investors and accredited investors who commit large amounts of money for long periods of time. In general, a private equity firm will raise a pool of capital, called a private equity fund, out of which it will make investments in specific companies. There are two main types of private equity firms: passive investors and active investors. Passive investors are entirely dependent on the company's management to grow the company. Active investors provide operational support to management to help build the company and increase profits.

In general terms, a private equity investment is a fixed equity investment that the investor is looking to obtain a return commiserate with its equity risk through a growth in cash flow, an increase in the multiple paid for those cash flows, or a combination thereof.

Insurance Companies

Insurance companies are a viable alternative for sources of debt capital. Life insurance companies are major lenders in the commercial and industrial mortgage market, the farm mortgage market, and the corporate bond market. These lenders allocate capital on a relative value basis in order to generate considerable earnings to support their insurance and annuity products.

401(k)s and Other Qualified Plans

In an ESOP transaction, one possible source of equity is the capital invested in financing existing 401(k) plans, IRAs and other qualified plans. The participants in qualified plans can agree to transfer funds to the ESOP, which the ESOP in turn can use to purchase equity from the company. Certain qualified plan assets such as 401(k) plan assets, profit-sharing plan balances, and IRA balances can be used in an ESOP transaction if allowed under the language of the applicable plan. These existing plan assets can be used only if all regulatory requirements are satisfied and an investment prospectus has been disclosed. There are no limits under federal securities laws on the amount of money in a qualified plan that can be transferred to an ESOP. Money voluntarily contributed to a qualified plan by an employee and transferred to the ESOP, however, generally cannot exceed certain limits based on the size of the transfer relative to the size of the company.

Management

Another possible source of equity is from the company's own management. Individuals on the company's management team can provide personal equity to help fuel a growth strategy or buy out an existing shareholder. This type of financing can be risky because this type of debt is subordinated to all other debt on the company's balance sheet. A management buyout is often used in conjunction with other debt instruments that can include senior financing, mezzanine financing, and seller financing. In a management buyout, the existing management's ownership interest is usually combined with personal wealth to provide the equity to purchase a portion or all of the equity from the sellers. In some situations, the management team may convert its current ownership interest into a seller note to help facilitate a 100% S corporation ESOP purchase.

Joint Venture

One way for two or more companies to partner and agree to share profit, loss, and control without having to merge is a joint venture. It is similar to a business partnership, with the difference that a partnership usually involves an ongoing, long-term business relationship, whereas a joint venture is based on a single business transaction. As the cost of starting new projects can be quite high, a joint venture allows both companies to share the burden of the project as well as the profits. A joint venture can offer a multitude of benefits to both parties through access to new resources, including financing, larger markets, distribution networks, capacity, purchasing power, and technology. All joint ventures are initiated by a contract between the participating parties, and this agreement specifies their mutual responsibilities and goals. The parties have the shared right to control the business unit, a right to share in the profits of the venture, and an obligation to share in any losses incurred.

Seller Financing

Seller financing is a loan provided by the seller of an asset or business to the buyer. This type of financing occurs when the buyer does not have sufficient equity to cover the purchase price or cannot qualify for a loan from a bank or other financial institution. High interest rates offered by financial institutions may also influence a buyer to engage in seller financing. Through seller financing, the buyer can usually make a down payment to the seller and then pay off the rest of the purchase price by making installment payments over a specified period at an agreed-upon interest rate. In most instances, the loan is secured by the property being sold. Because no institutional lenders are involved in the transaction, the overall terms of the financing are much more negotiable than would be through a bank. The buyer receives full title to the asset or business upon full repayment of the loan. If the buyer defaults on repaying the loan, the property is repossessed by the original seller.

Chapter 11

Seller Financing

Mary Josephs and Neal Hawkins

The use of seller financing has grown in recent years. In the earlier years of ESOPs, particularly before the advent of S corporation ESOPs, sellers bridged the gap between the company's enterprise value and its debt capacity by doing transactions in which the ESOP acquired only some percentage of the shares (often the company would do a number of these "staged" transactions to increase the ESOP ownership over time, often to 100%). The size of the ESOP could more or less be determined by debt capacity. The seller would sell whatever percentage the company could afford to finance with senior financing. While executing a smaller ESOP remains a solid strategy, many companies are taking time to evaluate the feasibility of becoming 100% ESOP-owned. Among other benefits, this enables the company to make a solid statement about employee ownership, remove the complexity of less-than-100% S corporation ESOPs, eliminate the need for costs associated with subsequent transactions, and realize increased tax benefits. Basic corporate finance teaches us the formula:

Enterprise Value = Debt Plus Equity

It is impossible to finance a non-ESOP company electing to pursue a 100% ESOP entirely with third-party debt (in the traditional form of senior and mezzanine capital). Lenders and ESOP trustees will require equity in transactions. This "equity" is often filled by having the selling shareholder provide financing through a deeply subordinated note. A compelling shareholder objective in ESOP transactions is to create a legacy, keep jobs in their community, and enable the company to perpetuate long after the shareholder is gone. While it is not a transaction requirement, more often than not, sellers prefer to minimize the third-party debt burden on the company. They prefer to support the success of the company by providing financing in lieu of the company borrowing from a higher-cost financing source, such as a mezzanine lender or private equity firm.

Design and Characteristics of Seller Financing

Design and Feasibility: Why Think About Seller Financing?

Seller notes are only one piece of the capital structure within the context of the entire transaction. As such, it is imperative to understand the seller's objectives to structure a successful transaction. As objectives will differ based upon each owner, it is a good practice to understand the different structuring and financing alternatives to help accomplish the objectives. During the feasibility and design stage, companies can compare different seller and third-party financing alternatives side-by-side and over time. This enables the company to make an informed decision. These alternatives should include both qualitative and quantitative data points as well as a sensitivity analysis. The quantitative data usually includes a payback analysis, the internal rate of return, company leverage, and tax implications. Many of the qualitative points are important issues identified by the seller and the management team (such as management succession or sustainability). Depending on the complexity of the situation and the company's familiarity with the myriad of ESOP and non-ESOP alternatives, external advisors (such as an investment bank, a consultant, or a lawyer) are hired to help model and present the different alternatives.

The more rigorous the pre-transaction analytics, including comparison of ESOP and non-ESOP alternatives, the more successful the transaction execution becomes. Although it is not necessarily intuitive to business owners comparing transaction alternatives, the ESOP often provides more cash to a shareholder over time than selling the company outright.

Structuring Considerations and Long-Term View

Seller notes can be structured in a number of different ways depending on the selling shareholder's objectives. Seller financing can provide the ESOP company flexibility when compared to other alternative debt options, such as mezzanine debt, which may require more cash interest payment on a yearly basis. Seller financing securities are debt (notes with interest and warrants) and must meet appropriate tests to be classified as debt, including a minimum rate of interest known as the applicable federal rate (AFR), a floating rate set by the IRS, a date certain of maturity, and other terms and conditions. There can be more than one tranche of seller notes, each with a unique design. The selling shareholder and the company have to understand and plan for the fact that any deferred payment, either through the use of PIK interest or through the use of warrants, most likely will be a cash obligation in the future. Long-term capital planning and strategic analysis on how the capital structure affects the company, the company's debt capacity, the ESOP, and the selling shareholders is crucial to ensuring the sustainability of an ESOP.

Seller Notes: Benefits and Considerations for the Seller

While seller notes do provide flexibility for the company, the holder of the seller note has to first understand that he or she will be subordinate to any other lenders (i.e., senior banks or mezzanine lenders). These institutions will require the seller notes to be structurally and legally subordinated, limiting the rights for the seller note holders. Senior lenders will have a priority lien on the assets and have the ability to block cash interest payments on the seller notes if the company fails to meet certain covenants set forth by the senior lender. In cases when cash interest is blocked, the company should be able to accrue the interest to the seller notes. Senior lenders will require that the seller note maturity be beyond that of their note(s). Given the deep subordination, most lenders will also prohibit any amortization or payment on the seller notes without written approval. In some instances, a senior lender may allow some prepayment of the seller notes based on performance hurdles and allowing a portion of excess free cash flow to be applied to the seller note principal. Seller note terms and conditions generally do not have typical market provisions other junior capital providers may require, such as drag along/tag along, cross-default, or standstill provisions.

Seller Notes: Benefits and Considerations for the Company

It is the duty of the company's board of directors and CFO to understand the implications and benefits of seller notes as a form of capital. Management needs to understand that while seller notes can provide flexibility, there are drawbacks. Seller notes are debt instruments. They do need to be repaid to meaningfully create long-term equity appreciation. The key analytical question for a company is whether the projections and related sensitivity analysis give comfort that, over time, the company can redeem the seller notes and grow meaningful share value for employee-owners' retirement accounts.

Return Characteristics for Seller Financing

For the note holder, the all-in return comes from two separate components: interest (both cash and paid-in-kind) and warrants. The mix between these components will determine the risk and return for the note holder. The interest is the fixed part of the return, while the warrant provides a variable and more risky return as it is tied to the future equity growth.

Paid-in-Kind Versus Cash Interest

Paid-in-kind (PIK) interest[1] is a unique tool to lessen the cash interest obligation paid by the company, relieving some stress on current cash flow. If interest is PIK (instead of cash), the unpaid interest is added to the principal of the note. PIK is used commonly to provide a company with cash flow flexibility, minimizing the required cash need on the company in the near-term in exchange for paying at a later period. PIK interest can apply either to the entire rate charged or, more frequently, to a portion of the interest. For example, an interest rate on a seller note might be 10%, of which 3% is cash and 7% is PIK.

While the increased flexibility of using PIK interest over traditional current-pay interest is attractive, it does come at a cost to the company and the selling shareholder. The company should understand,

---

1. PIK interest is interest that is accrued to the principal (added to the outstanding loan balance) instead of being paid in cash, thus being paid at maturity.

through longer-term capital analysis, the total cost that can, unfettered, exceed the future debt capacity of the company, suppress value accretion for the ESOP, and ultimately force a sale or liquidation (all being unintended consequences). Figure 11-1 shows the impact of compounding interest from PIK interest compared to cash interest over a 10-year period.

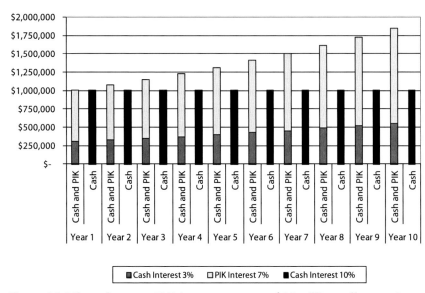

Figure 11-1 (based upon a 10% interest rate on a $10 million seller note)

Figure 11-1 shows that over a 10-year period the 7% PIK interest will compound dramatically, with the balance of the seller note increasing from $10 million to over $18.4 million. To provide some context, if the PIK rate were increased by 3% to 10%, the principal balance of the seller note would grow to $23.6 million—over 2.4 times the original seller note balance for the 10-year period. This is the power of compounding interest that needs to be considered when using PIK interest. A look at the cumulative cost of financing as shown in figure 11-2 highlights the 38% cost increase.

Figure 11-2 shows the cumulative effect of PIK and cash interest compared to the cash-only interest over the 10-year period. The total amount of cash and PIK interest paid was $13.8 million, or $3.8 million more than the cumulative cash interest paid. The additional $3.8 million might not seem like a lot at first blush, but that is value not being allocated to ESOP participant accounts. A trustee will also calculate the effective interest rate (or the annual interest rate based upon the total amount of interest over the life of the loan) for the loan based upon the total amount of cash and PIK interest paid, which in this case would have been 13.8%.

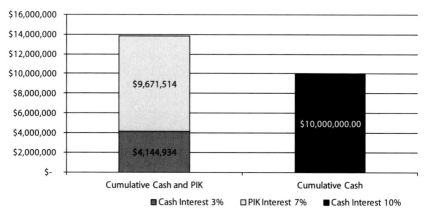

Figure 11-2

Companies should understand and weigh the benefits and considerations of using PIK interest with a seller note. In a default occurs, a senior lender will require any cash interest paid on the seller financing to instead be paid in PIK until such time as the borrower emerges from default. Absent care and thoughtful planning at the outset, PIK interest could significantly decrease ESOP benefits.

Warrants

A warrant is a security that, similarly to a call option, allows the holder to buy the company's stock at a specified price until a specified expiration date. Most businesses are familiar with debt, leases, and perhaps even swaps (interest-rate hedges) as financial securities. Each has a purpose and a unique design to accomplish the financial purpose. Warrants are usually issued in conjunction with a debt instrument. Debt holders require compensation for the risk of lending. With traditional lenders, the compensation is interest expense. For junior debt, arguably more risky as it is unsecured and subordinated to senior bank credit, traditional interest-only compensation is not sufficient relative to the risk. Warrants allow note holders to enhance their security return commensurate with the risk. Warrants are commonly issued in ESOP transactions as part of the economic value provided to the individuals providing subordinated seller financing. Seller financing will be subordinated to a senior lender and potentially a mezzanine lender. Given the deep subordination of the seller notes, warrants compensate the seller for providing junior capital needed to complete the transaction.

Warrants from the Lender's Perspective

Seller financing has two distinct advantages from a senior capital provider's point of view: enhanced cash flow available for debt service and a lower leverage multiple of total funded debt.

Cash flow available for debt service is critical to determining debt capacity. The fewer claims on cash flow, the more readily a company can meet debt service. ESOP companies are often equally concerned with not overburdening their balance sheets. Returns on junior capital are traditionally in two forms: (1) current-pay predetermined cash interest and (2) equity-type returns contingent on the financial performance of the company. Traditional junior capital (this is market driven) generally has a requirement for current interest of 10% to 12%. This is significantly greater than the level of current-pay interest often required by sellers, who can be comfortable with receiving much of their return in the form of warrants.

Looking back to figure 11-1, for a $10 million mezzanine investment the cash interest burden would vary considerably based upon the financing source chosen. Traditional junior capital might cost the company between $1 million and $1.2 million in interest expense, based on a rate of 10% to 12%, versus $300,000 to $400,000 in interest expense for seller financing, based on a rate of 3% to 4%.

The credit markets rely heavily on senior debt and total debt covenants. Any third-party junior capital will be included in the total debt covenant by a senior lender. For lenders familiar with ESOPs, seller financing can be underwritten as equity and not count within the total leverage covenant. When the company is an S corporation, these banks understand that use of seller financing to achieve 100% ESOP ownership will improve cash flow to repay debt as a result of the company being tax-exempt. As previously mentioned, the lender will also prohibit any amortization of the seller note and in a default would be able to stop cash interest payments indefinitely, both of which provide additional comfort to a senior lender.

Warrants from the Company's Perspective

As with any other current or long-term obligation, companies must carefully analyze warrants or other types of synthetic equity. The benefit of warrants to the company is clear. By moving a large portion of the seller note return from interest to warrants, companies can protect free cash flow (see the lender example above). Nonetheless, companies must understand the limitations, costs, and legal rules related to warrants.

Fairness and anti-abuse issues: The IRS and DOL carefully monitor fairness to all parties in ESOP transactions. One must follow both the fairness standards and the anti-abuse rules under Section 409(p) of the Internal Revenue Code when designing warrants for S corporation ESOPs. From a fairness perspective, seller notes cannot have projected returns greater than prevailing market returns for similar securities. For example, if there were a seller note that, given the risk and total leverage for a particular company, would likely bear an internal rate of return (IRR) of 14% in the open market, the IRR on that seller note should be at or below 14% (generally ESOP securities are priced slightly to significantly below market). One could not legally, using this example, structure a seller note with 4% current pay and a warrant with a projected yield suggesting an IRR of 18%. The S corporation ESOP anti-abuse rules are equally important. When structuring S corporation ESOP transactions, warrants and other synthetic equity cannot dilute the ESOP below 50% economic ownership. Additionally, the security design of the seller note cannot look so much like equity that it constitutes a second class of stock, since S corporations can have only one class of stock.

Short-term and long-term costs: Warrants have a set strike price when issued. Any price increase between the strike price and the price at which the warrant is redeemed is the obligation of the company. Depending on the structure, the warrant may be settled with stock or cash. Settling the warrant for stock makes a company that was 100% ESOP-owned now only partially ESOP-owned. Typically, the warrant is settled in cash. The company, using company cash or a new senior facility, buys back the warrant from the holder(s) at the fair market rate less the strike price. 100% ESOP-owned S corporations have a strong incentive to buy back the warrant. If the warrant holder becomes a shareholder, he or she (1) must be a valid S corporation shareholder and (2) will likely need tax distributions for his or her pro rata share of ownership. The company would no longer be 100% exempt from federal income taxes. Long-term planning is advised so the company can plan for this liability. Warrants generally mature after the original transaction financing has been repaid, a time when companies have sufficient debt cash and/or debt capacity for the redemption.

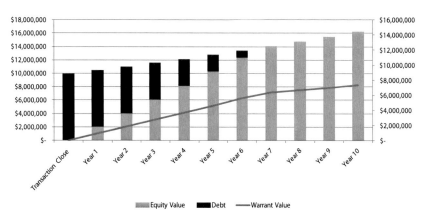

Figure 11-3. Ten-year warrant appreciation

Figure 11-3 provides an example of a $10 million ESOP transaction over a 10-year period. This example shows how quickly equity value is created in the early years of an ESOP, which is driven by the debt repayment and overall profit growth. The warrant value (shown by the line) increases in step with the equity value and over a 10-year period grows from having little value to being worth over $7.0 million.

Warrants from the Selling Shareholder's Perspective

Sellers providing seller financing should understand the advantages and considerations of this investment decision. Advantages of the warrant include a continued opportunity to participate in the equity appreciation of the company after the transaction, providing the company less onerous terms than third-party junior capital, reducing the cash-pay interest burden to the company, and providing the ability to be taxed at capital gains rates when it is settled in the future, compared to receiving interest that is taxed as ordinary income under current rules. There are also many estate and gift tax planning strategies that can be used with warrants. On the other hand, the return from a warrant is less certain than the return from structured interest. If the company does not continue to grow, the warrants could be valueless. Governance is a consideration for selling shareholders with continued investment in the company. As is common with mezzanine and junior capital providers, seller note holders may require that they remain on the board of directors and retain some continued governance rights while they retain capital in the company.

The warrant aligns the selling shareholder's interest with those of the ESOP and its participants because the seller will still have an equity stake after the transaction. The warrant should provide some comfort from the ESOP point of view because the selling shareholder is exchanging a portion of the guaranteed interest rate for the uncertainty of equity growth. The reduced interest rate is also beneficial to the ESOP because the interest expense will free up more cash, which can be used to pay down debt or reinvest back into the company, helping to increase the equity value for all participants. As the value of the warrant is driven by equity growth, the ESOP has created an incentive directly tied to creating value for its participants—the greater the ESOP equity, the more valuable the warrant.

Conclusion

With full understanding of the nuances involved for the company, the ESOP, and the seller, seller financing may be the optimal strategy to meet the owner's objectives. When owners are looking at a gradual ownership exit, a seller note might be the appropriate solution. Seller financing, like other structuring considerations for ESOP feasibility, needs to be looked at holistically, benchmarking the pros and cons in light of the shareholders' long-term objectives.

Financial Glossary

Mary Josephs and Neal Hawkins

Advance Rates: The percentage of book or appraised value a lender will apply for a given asset. Advance rates are dependent on the underlying asset and vary from zero to 100%. A lender will apply the applicable advance rates to a set of assets to determine the asset coverage of a specific loan. A lender will also remove stale or unsalable assets before applying the advance rate; these types of assets can include receivables greater than 90 days old, work in progress, or specialized assets, to name a few.

Asset Valuation: Depending on the type of asset being pledged, a lender may require the asset to be valued by an appraiser. The types of assets that are most commonly appraised are property and equipment but can include other valuable assets. An appraiser will usually provide different types of valuation in the analysis, which could include the fair market value, orderly liquation value, and forced liquidation value. Depending on the type of asset and the industry, a lender usually applies an advance rate against one of the asset valuations.

Best Efforts: See "Underwriting."

Blanket Lien: A legal first right to all assets of a borrower as collateral for a loan obligation. Blanket liens are most commonly required with most senior lenders who require a first priority to the assets of the borrower.

Club Deal: See "Underwriting."

Credit Underwriting: See "Underwriting."

Commitment Letter: A formal commitment from a lender or investor to provide financing or an investment based upon the terms and conditions disclosed. Commitment letters are the formal legal process of finalizing a term sheet.

Covenant: A requirement for a borrower to meet certain metrics in a predetermined time frame. Covenants allow a lender to receive warning signs of a borrower's decrease in performance. Typically, covenants are tested on a quarterly or annual basis and can include leverage covenants (i.e., senior debt/EBITDAE or total debt/EBITDAE) and/or cash flow covenants (i.e., minimum EBITDA, fixed charge coverage ratio; see below).

EBITDA: Commonly defined as earnings before interest, taxes, depreciation, and amortization. EBITDA is a common metric that is used to measure cash flow of a borrower. A lender will use this metric to measure or underwrite the amount of debt can be provided to a borrower and the risk of that borrower. A lender will usually also include a cash flow or leverage covenant that is tied to the EBITDA (such as a minimum EBITDA or senior debt/EBITDA).

EBITDAE: EBITDA plus ESOP financing costs (i.e., interest and principal on non-cash ESOP expense) that negatively affect a company's income statement. This term is frequently used to measure an ESOP company's cash flow.

Field Audit: An in-person inspection of the assets pledged to a senior lender. Field audits allow a lender to validate the accuracy of the inventory, receivables, and payables of a borrower. Field exams are usually preformed in conjunction with asset-based loans on an annual or semiannual basis.

Floating Rate: An interest rate that is subject to change based upon an underlying rate (i.e., LIBOR or prime).

Firm Underwriting: See "Underwriting."

Fixed Charge Coverage Ratio: A common ratio defined as a company's cash flow (usually defined as EBITDAE) divided by corresponding fixed charges (interest, amortization, capital expenditures, etc.) for a specific period. The ratio measures a borrower's cash inflow to the cash outflow for fixed expenses.

Fixed Rate: An interest rate that is constant for the life of a loan.

High-Yield Bond: A bond with a speculative credit rating of BB (S&P) or Ba (Moody's) or lower. Junk or high-yield bonds offer investors higher yields than bonds of financially sound companies. Two agencies, Standard & Poors and Moody's Investor Services, provide the rating systems for companies' credit. High-yield bonds are seen as riskier investments demanding a higher yield. From a lender's vantage point, the borrowing costs would increase when a borrower is deemed to fall within this speculative rating.

Inside Loan: A loan between the ESOP trust and the sponsor company in a leveraged ESOP. The inside loan is paid down over time with contributions from the sponsor company.

Institutional Lenders: Entities such as investment companies or funds, mutual funds, insurance companies, pension funds, and endowments with large amounts of capital to invest in unrelated businesses. These institutional lenders can be accessed by a borrower, usually through a private placement. Private placements can be a source of stable capital for a borrower and usually provide greater flexibility than a traditional senior lender.

Inter-Creditor Agreement: A legal agreement between senior creditors and subordinated creditors regarding the rights of each party. Inter-creditor agreements usually limit subordinated holders' rights in a default scenario, protecting the senior lender's ability to recover its investment or loan.

Junk Bond: A bond with a speculative credit rating of BB (S&P) or Ba (Moody's) or lower. Junk or high-yield bonds offer investors higher yields than bonds of financially sound companies. Two agencies, Standard & Poors and Moody's Investor Services, provide the rating systems for companies' credit. Junk bonds are seen as riskier investments demanding a higher yield. From a lender's vantage point, the borrowing costs increase when a borrower is deemed to fall within this speculative rating.

Leverage Covenant: A covenant calculation usually defined as senior debt outstanding divided by EBITDAE or total debt outstanding divided by EBITDAE. In general, a leverage covenant will measure the number of times a company's current cash flow has been leveraged (e.g., a 4x leverage covenant would dictate that it would take 4 years of existing cash flow to repay the debt).

LIBOR: London Interbank Offered Rate. LIBOR is a common floating interest rate index that lenders use as a base rate to calculate interest. For a borrower, LIBOR interest rate pricing is usually the base rate plus a spread (e.g., LIBOR + 200 basis points).

Personal Guarantee: A pledge of an owner's personal assets as collateral for a loan obligation. Personal guarantees are used to supplement the blanket lien on all corporate assets. In most situations, personal guarantees are required when there is a shortfall of assets at the company. Personal guarantees are usually found in smaller transactions and are used to decrease the risk of a credit. Personal guarantees can pose a problem in transactions where all the equity will be held by an ESOP, given that a trustee cannot provide a guarantee.

PIK Interest: Interest that is paid in kind (PIK) or accrued to the principal instead of being paid in cash. PIK interest is added to the outstanding loan balance. PIK interest is used to provide a borrower with cash flow flexibility in the short term and is usually assigned to subordinated debt. PIK interest is also used as a secondary source of payment if a borrower falls into default. In a default, a senior lender will require any subordinated cash interest to be converted into PIK interest to protect its senior investment. PIK interest has to be carefully understood because the compounding nature of the interest will require a larger payment at a future date.

Pledge: An agreement from a borrower to do or provide something. It is also an item (such as an asset) that is delivered as security in exchange for a loan and can be subject to being lost if the agreement is not fulfilled. In almost all loan agreements, the borrower will pledge to repay the debt and interest according to an agreed-upon schedule.

Pro-Rata Lender: A lender that purchases a fixed percentage of all tranches of a company's debt, including the revolver and all term loans. Pro-rata hold positions are used in club and syndicated transactions. An example of a pro-rata lender would be a lead bank that committed to 50% of the financing and provided half of the revolver commitment and half of the term loans.

Mezzanine: A loan obligation that is subordinated to a senior lender and usually has a secondary claim or possibly no claim at all to the assets of a borrower. A mezzanine lender has a lower priority than other, more senior lenders, but a greater priority than equity holders in liquidation. Given this increased risk, a mezzanine lender will require a greater return. This return usually is provided in the form of a cash interest rate and an equity interest. With ESOPs, mezzanine debt is usually used when a seller requires the maximum amount of cash at closing.

Negative Pledge: A legal obligation prohibiting a borrower from an action; i.e., a pledge in which the borrower agrees not to do something. The lender will impose various negative pledges to avoid actions that would undermine the business or affect the lender's security. For example, common negative pledges can include prohibiting the borrower from entering into any additional liens or prohibiting a borrower from acquiring another company without lender approval.

Revolver: A loan commitment from a bank or other financial institution that can be drawn upon at the borrower's discretion with no set amortization. Revolvers are most commonly used to help finance working capital needs of a company.

Second Lien: A senior lender that has secondary priority to an asset or group of assets. Second liens can include Term B loans or second mortgages. A second lien is mainly used with stable borrowers who are trying to maximize senior leverage and is usually priced slightly higher than traditional senior leverage. Second-lien loans can also be used in situations when a borrower would like to obtain flexible amortization on senior debt through a Term B loan.

Seller Note: A specific type of financing, usually subordinated to senior lenders, which is provided by the selling shareholders in a transaction. The selling shareholders take a debt obligation in exchange for the sale of their equity.

Senior Debt: Financing that is provided by banks and non-bank financial institutions that have a first lien or priority on the assets of a borrower. Senior debt is usually the most cost-effective capital for a borrower.

Springing Lien: A legal right that is instated when a borrower's performance falls below a predetermined level or when a borrower's leverage increases beyond a predetermined level. A springing lien is usually found with a larger borrower where a lender can gain comfort with the predictability of future cash flows.

Stock Appreciation Right: A form of synthetic equity that allows the owner of the security a right in the equity appreciation above the predetermined exercise price.

Subordinated Debt: A subordinated debt obligation has lower priority than other outstanding debt obligations.

Swap: A financial tool that allows a borrower to convert a payment from a floating rate to a fixed rate, or vice versa. A swap is most commonly used with senior debt to convert the interest rate payment from a floating rate (LIBOR plus a spread) to a fixed rate. The interest rate environment, tenure of the swap (e.g., the number of years the swap is outstanding), and macroeconomics will dictate the cost to a borrower to swap the interest payment.

Syndication/Syndicate: See "Underwriting."

Term A: A term loan, typically from a bank, requiring interest payments and principal amortization (typically over a five- to seven-year period).

Term B: A term loan from a bank or other financial institution requiring interest payments and modest principal amortization while Term A loans are being amortized. Term B loans typically amortize rapidly in the years following the scheduled repayment of the Term A loan.

Term Loan: A loan, usually provided by a financial institution, for a specific dollar amount with a certain date of maturity that requires the borrower to repay the borrowings over a predetermined schedule.

Unitranche: A type of loan that combines characteristics of senior financing and junior debt into one facility. A unitranche facility usually provides a blended rate between the senior and junior financing markets.

Underwriting: The process in which a lender will conduct due diligence on a prospective buyer to understand its business, financial performance, and management team. A lender will need to understand the use of the loan or investment and repayment of principal and interest. For a borrower, it is an opportunity to educate the lender or investor on its market position and competitive advantages. The lender will use the information gathered and look to compare the market conditions of similar-sized loans or investments for price, terms, and conditions.

- *Syndication/Syndicate:* A group of lenders or investors that combine their assets to lend to a borrower. Syndications allow lenders the ability to diversify credit exposure away from any single borrower. Usually the syndicate will have one bank take the lead or agent effort on coordinating the loan process. For a borrower, a syndicate allows the company to reduce its dependence on a single capital provider. In addition, the syndicate may have the ability to provide additional loans or investments for future capital needs.

Types of underwriting include both single-creditor and syndication arrangements. Examples of syndication underwritings include:

- *Best Efforts:* A method of syndicating (see above) a loan facility through which one lender (often called the "lead bank") agrees to use its best efforts to source all the capital providers needed for a borrower's debt facilities. The borrower retains the risk of insufficient capital or varying terms and conditions if the lead bank is not successful on its best efforts to source the agreed-upon capital. Best efforts underwriting is helpful for borrowers who do not have sufficient relationships with or knowledge of capital providers to meet their needs. While pricing for all forms of loan syndications is market-driven and varies over time, generally speaking, best efforts underwriting will be less expensive than a firm underwriting and more expensive than a club deal.

- *Club Deal:* A bank financing involving three or more banks in which no single bank takes a formal lead in structuring the transaction. Rather, in a club deal, the CFO will leverage relationships with other banks to bring together the group of capital providers. The banks will work together to structure a mutually acceptable financing package for the benefit of the borrower. In most cases, one bank will be designated to be the agent or lead bank to negotiate legal documents.

- *Firm Underwriting:* A firm underwriting is one in which a lender commits to fund an entire debt facility, bearing a syndication risk related to the financing (i.e., taking the risk that it will be able to find other lenders to purchase part of its position as a lender in a given financing at the agreed-to price, terms, and conditions promised the borrower). Firm underwriting is helpful when a borrower needs to close a transaction. Sometimes a single bank will fund the entire transaction and seek to fill the bank syndicate after closing. If the amount, terms, conditions, and timing of capital are critical to a particular transaction, a borrower may consider the value in a firm underwriting. Because of the increased risk a lender is taking, firm underwritings generally have higher fees and interest rates than those under club deals or best-efforts syndications. Most lenders have "market out" clauses that protect the underwriter in the event of a significant market shift during the underwriting process. This means that if there is a capital markets shift during a firm underwriting process, the lender is relieved of the firm commitment to the underwriting.

About the Authors

Vaughn Gordy is the chairman of the board and chief executive officer of GreatBanc Trust Company's Qualified Retirement Plans Services Group and has 17 years' experience in the ESOP trustee business. Mr. Gordy is also an author and speaker on many ESOP issues as well as a member of the ESOP Association, the National Center for Employee Ownership (NCEO), and Employee-Owned S Corporations of America (ESCA).

Neal Hawkins is a vice president at Verit Advisors. He began his career at LaSalle Bank, NA (now Bank of America Merrill Lynch), where he worked to help syndicate debt financing for complex middle-market transactions. Mr. Hawkins gained deeper investment banking experience at LaSalle Corporate Finance (now Bank of America Merrill Lynch) while advising middle-market companies on various corporate finance solutions, including leveraged buyouts, mergers, acquisitions, recapitalizations, and ESOPs. He then was the national ESOP consultant and vice president in Bank of America's ESOP Solutions Group, advising business owners and management teams on implementing ESOPs as a transition alternative. In addition to helping structure new ESOPs, Mr. Hawkins was responsible for working with existing ESOP companies to provide strategic advice on capital structures and financing alternatives. Mr. Hawkins holds a BS in finance from Northern Illinois University and is currently pursuing his MBA at Kellogg School of Management. Mr. Hawkins is on the Finance Committee for the ESOP Association. He is a member of FINRA and holds Series 7 and 63 licenses.

Mary Josephs is the founder and CEO of Verit Advisors. Ms. Josephs has more than 28 years of experience with ESOPs. She has advised, structured and closed more than 200 financings for middle-market companies, representing more than $7 billion in senior credit and nearly $30 billion in enterprise value, most of which have supported ESOP transactions. Ms. Josephs founded and built the ESOP group at LaSalle

National Bank and cofounded and launched a leading ESOP advisory practice for ABN AMRO LaSalle Corporate Finance (subsequently Bank of America-Merrill Lynch). Ms. Josephs has also held leadership positions throughout the ESOP community, serving as chair of the Finance Advisory Committee of the ESOP Association (TEA), as a member of TEA's board of directors, as an NCEO board member, as an advisory board member for Employee-Owned S Corporations of America, as chair of TEA's advisory committees, and as a lifetime member of TEA's board of governors. Ms. Josephs has spoken at hundreds of conferences nationally and frequently writes on issues related to succession and liquidity alternatives for closely held businesses. She holds a BA in economics and French from Marquette University and an MBA in finance from the University of Chicago's Booth School of Business.

William W. Merten is a partner in the law firm of McDermott Will & Emery LLP and is based in the firm's Chicago office. He focuses his practice on business succession planning and executive compensation. Mr. Merten frequently speaks regarding tax-advantaged liquidity and succession issues for various organizations. He has in the past been an executive compensation professor for DePaul University's Masters of Law in Taxation program and a qualified plan professor for DePaul's Masters of Science in Taxation program. He previously also served on DePaul's Masters of Law (in Taxation) Advisory Committee. Mr. Merten has authored or coauthored articles and chapters for various publications regarding sales and exchanges, mergers and acquisitions, executive compensation techniques, corporate reorganizations, liquidations, installment sales, and tax procedures. He received a BA degree (with high honors) from Michigan State University, a JD from Wayne State University, and an LLM in taxation from New York University.

Rebecca (Becky) Miller has nearly 40 years of public accounting experience. She first was a sole practitioner, then was with one of the major international accounting firms, and for the last 30-plus years has been with McGladrey & Pullen. During this time she has focused on employee benefit tax, audit, accounting, and operational issues. This has included direct client service and two stints in McGladrey's national tax office. She has served as a leader in McGladrey's employee benefit plan consulting practice and most recently as part of the employee benefit plan audit team in McGladrey's National Professional Standards Group. She worked on her first ESOP transaction in 1976 and continues to work on ESOPs. She is the only member of the American Institute of Certified Public Accountants (AICPA) task force responsible for the drafting of the ESOP accounting standard who remains in active practice in this arena. In 2012, she served as a technical advisor to the AICPA's Employee Benefit Plans Audit Quality Center as it worked to draft a primer for auditors of ESOP plans.

Scott Rodrick is the director of publishing and information technology at the National Center for Employee Ownership (NCEO). He designed and created the NCEO's present line of publications and is the author or coauthor of several books himself, including the best-selling *An Introduction to ESOPs* (13th ed. 2012). Since 1994, he has created and maintained the NCEO's presence on the Internet. He is an attorney and served at the U.S. Department of Labor as an attorney-advisor before coming to the NCEO. Before law school, he earned a BA at the University of California, Davis and an MA at the University of California, Los Angeles.

Corey Rosen is the founder and former executive director of the National Center for Employee Ownership (NCEO) and now is its senior staff member. He cofounded the NCEO in 1981 after working for five years as a professional staff member in the U.S. Senate, where he helped draft legislation on employee ownership plans. Before that, he taught political science at Ripon College. He is the author or coauthor of over 100 articles and many books on employee ownership, and a coauthor (with John Case and Martin Staubus) of *Equity: Why Employee Ownership Is Good for Business* (Harvard Business School Press, 2005). He has lectured on employee ownership on six continents, has appeared frequently on CNN, PBS, NPR, MSNBC, and other network programs, and is regularly quoted in the *Wall Street Journal,* the *New York Times, BusinessWeek,* and other leading publications. He holds a PhD in political science from Cornell University.

John Solimine is a founding member and principal of Verit Advisors. He has 12 years of experience in investment banking and debt capital markets, particularly with middle-market companies and private equity sponsors in succession and liquidity transactions. Mr. Solimine began his career at LaSalle Bank, NA (now Bank of America Merrill Lynch), where he provided debt financing alternatives for leading middle-market financial sponsors and their portfolio companies. This involved the structuring, underwriting, and portfolio management of senior credit facilities in connection with leveraged buyouts, recapitalizations, and growth financings. He gained broad investment banking experience at Bear Stearns & Co. and Jefferies & Company in New York. Mr. Solimine later joined Equibase Capital Group, a Chicago-based real estate private equity firm, where he worked with sophisticated high-net-worth investors and leading institutional investors of the firm's private investment vehicles, broadening his experience in private equity and institutional fund management. Mr. Solimine received a BS in business administration from Loyola University Chicago and an MBA in finance, economics, and strategic management from the University of Chicago Booth School of Business. Mr. Solimine is a member of FINRA and holds Series 7 and 63 licenses.

About the NCEO

The National Center for Employee Ownership (NCEO) is widely considered to be the leading authority in employee ownership in the U.S. and the world. Established in 1981 as a nonprofit information and membership organization, it now has over 2,500 members, including companies, professionals, unions, government officials, academics, and interested individuals. It is funded entirely through the work it does.

The NCEO's mission is to provide the most objective, reliable information possible about employee ownership at the most affordable price possible. As part of the NCEO's commitment to providing objective information, it does not lobby or provide ongoing consulting services. The NCEO publishes a variety of materials on employee ownership and participation; holds dozens of seminars, Webinars, and conferences on employee ownership annually; and offers a variety of online courses. The NCEO's work includes extensive contacts with the media, both through articles written for trade and professional publications and through interviews with reporters. It has written or edited several books for outside publishers. The NCEO's Web site is www.nceo.org.

NCEO Membership Benefits

- The bimonthly newsletter *Employee Ownership Report*, which covers ESOPs, equity compensation, and employee participation, plus our PDF-only newsletter *Equity Compensation Report.*

- Access to the members-only area of the NCEO's Web site, which includes a searchable newsletter archive, a discussion forum, a database of service providers, and more.

- Substantial discounts on publications, online courses, and events produced by the NCEO.

- Free access to live Webinars on both ESOPs and equity compensation.

- The right to contact the NCEO for answers to general or specific questions regarding employee ownership.

An introductory NCEO membership costs $90 for one year ($100 outside the U.S.) and covers an entire company at all locations, a single professional offering services in this field, or a single individual with a business interest in employee ownership. Full-time students and faculty members who are not employed in the business sector may join at the academic rate of $40 for one year ($50 outside the U.S.).

Selected NCEO Publications

The NCEO offers a variety of publications on all aspects of employee ownership and participation. Following are descriptions of a few of our main publications. We publish new books and revise old ones on a yearly basis. To obtain the most current information on what we have available, visit our extensive Web site at www.nceo.org or call us at 510-208-1300.

Employee Stock Ownership Plans (ESOPs)

- *Leveraged ESOPs and Employee Buyouts* combines a discussion of legal, accounting, and valuation issues with an extensive discussion of leveraged ESOP financing.

  $25 for NCEO members, $35 for nonmembers

- *Understanding ESOPs* is a general overview of the issues involved in establishing and operating an ESOP.

  $25 for NCEO members, $35 for nonmembers

- *Selling Your Business to an ESOP* focuses on the concerns of closely held businesses that are considering an ESOP sale, including the Section 1042 tax-deferred rollover.

  $25 for NCEO members, $35 for nonmembers

- *S Corporation ESOPs* introduces the reader to how ESOPs work and then discusses the legal, valuation, administrative, and other issues associated with S corporation ESOPs.

  $25 for NCEO members, $35 for nonmembers

- *Executive Compensation in ESOP Companies* discusses executive compensation issues, special ESOP considerations, and a survey of executive compensation in ESOP companies.

  $25 for NCEO members, $35 for nonmembers

- *The ESOP Company Board Handbook* is a guide for board members in ESOP companies.

  $25 for NCEO members, $35 for nonmembers

- *Don't Do That* is a guide to common mistakes in operating an ESOP and what to do about them.

  $25 for NCEO members, $35 for nonmembers

Equity Compensation Plans

- *The Decision-Maker's Guide to Equity Compensation* explains how equity compensation plans work and what the considerations are for choosing and designing them.

  $25 for NCEO members, $35 for nonmembers

- *Equity Alternatives: Restricted Stock, Performance Awards, Phantom Stock, SARs, and More* is a complete guide, including model plans, to phantom stock, restricted stock, stock appreciation rights, performance awards, and more.

  $35 for NCEO members, $50 for nonmembers

- *Equity Compensation for Limited Liability Companies* describes how equity compensation works in an LLC and provides model plan documents.

  $25 for NCEO members, $35 for nonmembers

To join the NCEO as a member or to order any of our publications, visit us on the Web at www.nceo.org, use the order form on the following page, or call us at 510-208-1300. If you join at the same time you order publications, you will receive the members-only publication discounts.

Order Form

This book is published by the National Center for Employee Ownership (NCEO). You can order additional copies online at our Web site, www.nceo.org; by telephoning the NCEO at 510-208-1300; by faxing this page to the NCEO at 510-272-9510; or by sending this page to the NCEO at 1736 Franklin Street, 8th Floor, Oakland, CA 94612. If you join as an NCEO member with this order, or are already an NCEO member, you will pay the discounted member price for any publications you order.

Name

Organization

Address

City, State, Zip (Country)

Telephone   Fax   Email

Method of Payment: ❑ Check (payable to "NCEO")   ❑ Visa   ❑ M/C   ❑ AMEX

Credit Card Number

Signature   Exp. Date

Checks are accepted only for orders from the U.S. and must be in U.S. currency.

Title	Qty.	Price	Total

Tax: California residents add 9% sales tax (on publications only, not membership)	Subtotal $
Shipping: In the U.S., first publication $5, each add'l $1; elsewhere, we charge exact shipping costs to your credit card, plus a $10 handling surcharge; no shipping charges for membership	Sales Tax $
	Shipping $
Introductory NCEO Membership: $90 for one year ($100 outside the U.S.)	Membership $
	TOTAL DUE $